Writing to Grow

Writing to Grow

Keeping a Personal-Professional Journal

Mary Louise Holly

Kent State University

Heinemann
Portsmouth, New Hampshire

Heinemann Educational Books, Inc.
70 Court Street   Portsmouth, NH 03801
Offices and agents throughout the world

The publisher and author wish to thank those whose words and writings are quoted here for permission to reproduce them, and to the following for permission to quote from previously published works:

Pages 70–71: From Sylvia Ashton-Warner, *Teacher*. Copyright © 1963 by Sylvia Ashton-Warner. Reprinted by permission of Simon & Schuster, Inc.

Page 85: From *The Reflective Practitioner: How Professionals Think in Action* by Donald A. Schön. Copyright © 1983 by Basic Books, Inc. Reprinted by permission of Basic Books, Inc., Publishers.

Page 120: Reprinted from *To the Is-Land* by Janet Frame with permission of George Braziller, Publishers. Copyright © 1982 by Janet Frame.

Pages 120–21: From *Growing Up* by Russell Baker. Copyright © 1982 by Russell Baker. Reprinted by permission of Congdon & Weed, Inc.

Figure 11–3: From John Elliott, "Action Research: A Framework for Self-Evaluation in Schools," TIQL Working Paper No. 1, Cambridge Institute of Education. Reprinted by permission of the author.

Every effort has been made to contact the copyright holders for permission to reprint borrowed material. We regret any oversights that may have occurred and would be happy to rectify them in future printings of this work.

Library of Congress Cataloging-in-Publication Data

Holly, Mary Louise.
    Writing to grow : keeping a personal-professional journal / Mary Louise Holly.
      p. cm.
    Bibliography: p.
    Includes index.
    ISBN 0-435-08494-1
    1. Teachers—Diaries—Authorship. 2. Professional socialization.
    3. Diaries—Authorship. 4. Autobiography—Authorship. I. Title.
LB1775.H58 1989
371.1′0023—dc20

89-32195
CIP

Text designed by Marie McAdam; cover by Jenny Greenleaf.
Printed in the United States of America.
10   9   8   7   6   5   4   3   2   1

To Brian
(who doesn't keep a journal)
and
for Kate and John
(who do)

Writing, like life itself,
is a voyage of discovery.

Henry Miller

Contents

Preface

I think in writing ... we are questioning ourselves ... and I think that there is very little
precedent set for us to do that. Yet, I think when
we look at the whole concept of professional
growth, that's a piece of it. Yes, you have to
do it.

Jerry Johnson (primary teacher)

The term "teacher as researcher" was introduced by Lawrence Stenhouse
in his book *An Introduction to Curriculum Research and Development* in
1975. Since that time, the concept of teacher inquiry has continued to
gain attention so that now it figures prominently in program and course
development in both pre-service and in-service education. Action research
and the development of systematic ways to inquire into teaching have
become important as the everyday and special circumstances and processes of teaching and curriculum development are observed, described,
and questioned. Study of teachers' concepts, theories, and thinking, as
well as their careers and life histories, continues to expand. Case studies
using biographical and narrative methods are increasing as both the
teacher as person and the social and cultural contexts of schooling are
explored in greater depth. This book draws on research and writing in
these areas and is designed to help teachers and others in educational
fields to explore their practice. My purpose is to describe how writing
can be used for professional development and research; how keeping a
journal can facilitate observation, documentation, and reflection on current and past experiences, including one's life history and the social,
historical, and educational conditions that usher in the present. When
teachers capture their stories while the action is fresh, they, like Jerry

Johnson, are often provoked to wonder "Why did I do this?" or "Why did this happen?"

In this book, examples from diaries and journals (from beginning and experienced teachers, administrators, teacher-educators, and noted writers such as Virginia Woolf and Sylvia Ashton-Warner) are used to describe what can happen as we engage in journal writing. The book is based on a longitudinal research project entitled "Teacher Reflections on Classroom Life—An Empirical Base for Professional Development" (see Appendix A for abstract) and a study of beginning teachers who kept journals over a school year in order to describe their lives as teachers. It also grew out of ideas presented in a monograph, *Keeping a Personal-Professional Journal* (Holly 1983; 1987).

My curiosity with writing and growing began a long time ago, at about age seven, when my mother said "Write it down, Mary Louise. I have to write things down or I forget them." So I did, and do. And when I don't, I often forget them. Writing seems especially important in teaching because there are so many things to consider and to remember while we are concerned with facilitating the learning of others. Although writing has always seemed to help in implanting and connecting thoughts and information, only recently have I begun to understand why this is so (see chapter 6). As an art teacher I marveled at the stories children (and adults) told with their pictures and sculptures, at the ways they came to know and be through their creations. As a classroom teacher I was continually amazed by children's ability to use their imagination and construct life stories when given the opportunity and encouraged to write. My experiences and research in teacher education and professional development since 1973 have helped me to clarify in my own mind some of the ways in which writing can contribute to growing.

A journal is a personal document. The writer is usually the only audience. The journal excerpts presented here were shared with me, and some of them were also shared with other teachers. Teachers were asked to reflect on each day and to note meaningful recollections. Content, style, and organization were matters of personal choice. Because we went about writing in a nondirected way, we learned our lessons as we went along. We found that there are no hard and fast rules. Each of us must develop procedures and organization according to our own purposes and styles.

Most of the examples presented are of teachers writing, but the principles and processes hold for other educators, too. Journal writing can be useful in exploring the personal and professional dimensions of practice whether this practice is teaching, administration, or supervision. The underlying assumptions are the following:

- Conscious reflection and deliberation concerning students, curricula, oneself, and the profession are inherent in professional practice.

- Teaching is inquiry.
- Inquiry, curriculum development, analysis, and evaluation are inextricably related, ongoing, personal, professional, and collegial.
- Supporting learning and development in others can best be done by those who are engaged in similar processes (reflecting on their own work).
- Continuing transformation of perspective (growth) is enhanced by gaining distance from practice and exploring different dimensions of experience from different points of view.

The book is divided into two parts. Part One begins with descriptions of personal documents, their uses, and the people who keep them. After examining the log, diary, and journal, we look into the journals of three teachers. In the concluding chapters of Part One, writing is addressed as a form of communication that leads to many different kinds of journal writing. Part Two might be described as the methodological or practical part of the book because it invites the reader to write and provides many examples and suggestions for doing so. The emphasis is on practice as it emanates from, and acts as a catalyst for, theorizing. It contains information and suggestions on several practical matters in journal keeping: how to begin, what to write about, and exercises and methods for personal and collegial inquiry.

This book and the research on which it is based have benefited from the ideas, challenge, and encouragement of many people. Carol Toncar and Gene Wenninger from Research and Sponsored Programs at Kent State University and Rolf Lehming of what was in 1981–82 the National Institute of Education were especially supportive in consultation on two research grants that enabled me to obtain the time and resources necessary to study teacher professional development and journal writing. Support from Joanne Whitmore and my discussions with colleagues in early childhood education, especially Carol Bersani, have also been valuable. Rich Vacca suggested the title. Kate Hulbert, Steve Snyder, Jim Jenkins, Dick Hawthorne, Pat Balazs, Jane Applegate, Maggie MacLure, and Peter Stillman each read the manuscript in one form or another and offered cogent comments and criticism. Pseudonyms are given for journal excerpts in the text; they are actually from the work of Steve Snyder, Jim Jenkins, Linda Lee, Crysann Kelly, Kathy Erickson, Pat Balazs, Pat Little, Don Haren, Cynthia Vesia, Nanvette Nemick, Kelley Moles, Tricia Perry, Kathy Rothermel, and Jim McConnell. Louise Sause and Charles Blackman have influenced this work more than they would want to; and John Elliott, Jennifer Nias, John Smyth, and Jan Sturm have each provoked more cogitation than I would want. Colleagues at the Centre for Applied Research in Education (CARE), especially Lucila Haynes, provided the colleagueship and support necessary to complete the manuscript while I was on sabbatical at the University of East Anglia.

Roy Edelfelt's persistent questions about reflective writing continue to plague and enrich my thinking, as they have since 1979 when we first discussed the research on which this book is based. Had Helen Hulbert —librarian, teacher, scholar, and my mother—known what she set in motion back in 1953, and what her involvement in preparing this book would be, she would surely have suggested I take up tennis rather than writing. Without Brian Holly, there would have been no journal, no theorizing about it, and certainly no book about keeping one.

PART ONE

Logs, Diaries, Journals, and Teachers Who Keep Them

Perhaps we write toward what we will become from where we are.

May Sarton

"Learning stamps you with moments" wrote Eudora Welty (1984, 10), and it is in the act of expressing moments on paper that journal writers discover themselves. Reflective writing projects the journal writer into a greater awareness of the present. To John Dewey it meant becoming "aware," to Maxine Greene becoming "awake." Part One explores what reflective writing is and how it can be used by teachers.

SECTION I

Reflective Writing

How do I know what I think until I see what I say?

E. M. Forster

Documenting experience, or simply talking to yourself, is reason enough to keep a diary or journal. What are logs, diaries, and journals? Who keeps them and why? What are the benefits of reflective writing for educators?

CHAPTER 1

Why Reflect in Writing?

Men go gape at mountain peaks, at the bound-
less tides of the sea, the broad sweep of rivers,
the encircling ocean and the motions of the stars;
and yet they leave themselves unnoticed; they
do not marvel at themselves.

St. Augustine

Several years ago, Lewis Thomas, well-known medical scientist and author of *The Lives of a Cell* (1975), wrote a short article celebrating the
progress of mankind on earth. I remember little about the brief paper
save the idea that mankind has come a great distance in a short while.
If we measure ourselves by how far we still have to go, we will always
feel inadequate. But if we look at how far we have progressed, the outlook
is quite different. How many teachers marvel at themselves? As St. Augustine observed, we focus on things around us, but how often do we
look with wonder at ourselves, the children we teach, our profession?
What if, like Lewis Thomas, we were to look more closely at what we
have done, what we do, and what we can do—both individually and
collaboratively?

This book is about professional development. Its focus is on journal
writing and how educators can use it to explore and grow from experience
and reflection on practice. Several classroom teachers who learned to wonder on paper about themselves, their students, and their profession share
their experiences here. Real-life stories are documented in vignettes about
teaching. Embedded within them are assumptions, values, and theories
about teaching and learning, images of self and of the profession. More
captivating than any best-seller or television drama are the stories that
unfold over time in these classrooms.

In an "everyday" journal entry by Tom (Figure 1–1), we glimpse a
teacher's world. Here we find concern for the "hidden promise" of a child;
thoughts of another child, David, who died of cancer during the third

FIGURE 1–1
Journal Entry—Tom

Monday March 2nd.

A busy day, as always. Papers to have the mom run. Kids work to save for this Fridays Spring Conferences.

Scoop, my new kid, came back. He was gone for Thur. & Fri.. I missed him. I'm not sure why, some hidden promise I suppose. His birthday was a week ago. He said he didn't get anything cause his mom didn't have any money.

I've no records on this kid, he has C.P. but I don't know how bad. He is poor, He is unkept, His clothes are worn and not especially clean. He looks anemic and has a twisting of the arms movement, He tires easily. He slurs his talking, His uncombed whitish-blondish hair falls like a barn boys over his eyebrows.

I bought Scoop a book bag on Thursday. I was hoping he would like it. He loved it! He lit up like a Xmas tree. It so nice to see him smile. His vulnerability reminds me, especially his ungainly walk, of David Niesker. I've not thought of that poor lad for some time now. I sure hope Scoop's life has less bleak moments than poor Danny's did.

week of school; planning and appreciation for a mother volunteer; orchestrating examples of children's work for parent–teacher conferences; and all "the daily trivial, but often earthshaking events, which melt a teaching day into a dizzy haze." These become journal reflections as Tom sits writing after school on March 2.

REASONS FOR JOURNAL WRITING

Why keep a personal-professional journal? Though you will find many reasons throughout this book, here are some that Tom, a beginning teacher and journal writer, offers:

> The good thing about having to write a journal is that you actually do it. This is not unlike some lesson plans. By having to actually put down some lessons one starts to figure out how to carry them out. One also has a record to look back on if things do or don't work out. To extend or revise notes is later in order. One can only hold a couple of thoughts down at the same time. New information seems to edge out other short-term data before it has a chance to imprint into longer-term memory. By writing we have a great pulp memory bank—Hell, there's lots of paper!

Though these are good reasons for keeping a journal, they didn't occur to Tom until the end of his first day of journal writing. Earlier that September day, he felt quite differently: "I hate the idea of having to be told to put my thoughts down in a log/journal format."

Tom had been asked to keep a journal as part of a seminar for beginning teachers. He took the assignment seriously. He had entered teaching with enthusiasm and commitment. After working six years in a steel plant and running his own construction business for two years, he decided to become a teacher. He earned a master's degree in early childhood education and received certification to teach. Now, here he was, a kindergarten teacher. This is what happened on Tom's first day of writing:

> **8:10** . . . We're fifteen minutes late already. It's going to be a long day. I hope Josh's [his three-year-old son] normal separation anxiety won't be too taxing at Montessori school where I drop him off. Always one more kiss. One more hug. . . . The worst part is that I need them almost as bad as he does. A good day for sure!
>
> **8:20** Just ran out to the car twice to get the rest of my normal load (guitar, briefcase, folder, new pillows, etc.). . . . I usually walk

but this morn I ran because I had written on my blotter/desk pad that we had a teachers' meeting scheduled. Next week is the teachers' meeting.

This day is pictures!

8:40 Oh, wonderful—an announcement for a staff picture before the kidders arrive. I was so concentrated on not forgetting part of my bring-back-load that I forgot to dress up for my own picture. Wonderful . . . the purple shirt. . . .

9:00 I took the picture with the rest of the staff. They were all slicked up. Here I am, in this faded, short-collared, purple & yuk checkered shirt. . . .

9:15 I ducked into the office to run only one batch (52) of papers . . . to get a lead on the copy machine. . . . I rush down the hall figuring that maybe one or two of the buses are in. . . . I get stopped by three teachers directing me to the other kindergarten room to see Cathy. I thought of my wife Cathy but they were referring of course to Catherine, the shy, sensitive, little five-year-old sobbing her guts out.

Catherine needs a hug and a hold. Mr. Carter doesn't mind the wet shirt. It kind of feels warm and snuggly. And it is a crappy shirt. Within one minute the crisis is over. . . . She'll survive and hopefully won't be too puffy for the picture. The shirt couldn't be made worse on purpose!

4:30 Davey's Dad shows up unannounced & wants to talk about Davey's problem. Would I recommend a larger dose of Mellirill? Did I know about Davey's visits to the psychologist? Should he hold back the buying of presents for the child's misbehaviors? . . .

Tom's initial skepticism about keeping a journal is well founded. It does take time, effort, and energy, much like teaching. But what he found after writing for one day are six important reasons for keeping a personal-professional journal:

1. "You actually do it"—*Writing necessitates a time-out from the motion of a busy day.* Many professional tasks and opportunities go unachieved, but keeping a journal demands a time-out from the rush of activity, and it provides a tangible result.
2. *The writer "starts to figure out" the journal subjects and topics* as the writing proceeds; it brings him or her one step closer to acting on behalf of concerns discovered in the writing.
3. *There is "a record to look back on,"* so analysis and planning can follow. Tom found that Catherine became a frequent subject of his writing.

In addition to documenting her behavior and his efforts on her behalf, he notes which ideas fail and which succeed, and the circumstances surrounding them.

4. With a record of experience, *the writer can "extend or revise"* later. The next time Davey's dad talks with Tom, he can write additional details. The journal provides ongoing documentation for analysis and evaluation.

5. If most human beings can "only hold a couple of thoughts down at the same time" and "new information" can be overwhelming, how is a teacher to retain important information to make professional decisions? *The journal offers a way to sort through the multitude of demands and interactions to highlight the most important ones.* Reflective writing enables learning from experience by capturing selected pictures from the flow of events.

6. By writing and returning to what is written, *there is time for* what Tom referred to as *"imprinting"—making connections* that might otherwise be overlooked.

Not only is journal writing useful for chronicling practice, for reflecting on, analyzing, and planning experience, it can also deepen awareness of the present ("I need [a hug] almost as much as he does"). It is one thing to sense something and another to understand it. Perhaps the most general and important reason for keeping a personal-professional journal is that it helps the author to better understand him- or herself, teaching, and the nature of the profession itself.

TEACHING, PROFESSIONAL DEVELOPMENT, AND REFLECTION

There is no *Book of Teaching*; the teacher writes it along the way, drawing on learning from others, from theories and practices presented during teacher preparation; and, beyond these, from the everyday realities of the classroom. Teaching calls forth everything the teacher is: personal and professional experience, general background, education, ethics, intelligence, and creativity. Today, attention is increasingly focused on the person who teaches (perceptions, intentions, life history) as well as on the context (social, historical, educational, political) and environment (classroom, school, community) within which schooling takes place. Scholars point out that teaching is dynamic and developmental, that children grow and learn in subtle as well as obvious ways, and that as teachers and the contexts of schooling change, the intricate relationships and interactions involved in teaching and learning also change.

As our understanding of teaching changes, so do the possibilities for shaping the profession. What the profession and schooling become depends in large part on educators' influence. And if we, as educators, are to influence schooling through professional expertise, we must speak with knowledge, confidence, compassion, and skill. As Eisner (1985) suggests, we must be both connoisseurs and critics of practice.

Connoisseurship begins in wonder, in posing questions and acting on one's curiosity. While it retains this sense of searching, it also focuses and channels inquiry and develops into more systematic research. Journal writing, or the "great pulp memory bank" Tom alludes to, enables reflecting to be a deliberative process for appreciating the complexities and subtleties of practice.

Reflection. One cannot teach or plan without it. Teachers reflect in action. There are hundreds, perhaps thousands, of decisions each day that require reflection ("What did Sheila do last time this happened?" "Yesterday, I said . . ."). We reflect on past experience and speculate about the future ("What might happen if . . . ?"). Keeping a personal-professional journal can help to make professional knowledge accessible for linking with current circumstances. For example, as Tom writes about Catherine and other children in the classroom, he makes mental connections and notes patterns of behavior. He anticipates needs before they are noticeable. As he observes children's developmental characteristics and personal qualities, he learns how to integrate and adjust teaching and curricula to accommodate these children.

While reflection in action is part of teaching (Schön 1983), reflection after the fact enables Tom to gain insights for understanding development and learning in ways that are not otherwise possible. This is because many experiences are comprehensible only after they occur; the most important gains made with children are often the most difficult to see. The written word, like a camera, freezes the action and yields snapshots we can interpret and learn from.

EXPLORING PRACTICE THROUGH JOURNAL WRITING

In January 1981, seven teachers and I began a research project entitled "Teacher Reflections on Classroom Life—An Empirical Base for Professional Development" (see Appendix A). The purpose of the project was to explore links between teaching and professional development. How do teachers grow and learn as they teach? What circumstances and experiences influence and shape teaching and professional development? What are the teacher's joys and frustrations? Who is the person who

TABLE 1–1

Project Teachers

Name	Sex, Age	Grade	Years Experience	Degree/Year	School/Students' SES*
Jerry J.	M, 33	2	5	BA, 1976	Sub, high SES
Carole C.	F, 29	1	8	BA, 1972	Sub, mixed SES, mixed ethnic
Craig C.	M, 31	K	5	BA, 1972 MA, 1976	Sub, low SES
Kate M.	F, 46	K	15	BA, 1956 MA, 1978	Rural, mixed SES
Marcy C.	F, 40	4	6	BA, 1963	Rural, mixed SES
Ruth B.	F, 49	3	14	BA, 1968	Urban, low SES
Judy G.	F, 32	2	10	BA, 1971	Sub, low SES

*SES = Socioeconomic status

teaches? In what ways does the teacher's life history influence teaching? What do teaching and professional development mean to teachers?

The teachers came from seven school districts and taught from kindergarten through fourth grade levels (see Table 1–1). For over a year we kept journals (at the time we used the terms *diary* and *journal* interchangeably) and met weekly as a seminar group to discuss topics generated from both the journals and teaching. I was also a participant-observer in each teacher's classroom for approximately three hours every other week throughout the project.

Conscious reflection and writing, as it turned out, were not as easy as I had anticipated when I designed the project. Nor had I anticipated the potential significance of reflective writing and collegial discussion for teaching and professional development. Ruth conveys this in her journal:

Sometimes teaching is a lonely business—imagine saying that when you are so involved with people! Lonely in the sense of feelings—caring, frustrated ones maybe. You know that others must have felt the same frustrations you felt, but where are they? That's the beauty of the support group such as this. I think that if we did nothing further than this journal business—I would still write for the catharsis. Going back, I remember and understand how I felt. And I feel a better person and teacher for the writing. . . .

This writing, and reviewing our writing is surprisingly educational. I thought I was knowledgeable about myself. I keep finding facets I didn't realize existed. . . .

During the last seminar session I asked the participants to write briefly about major aspects of the project: the observations, seminar, and journal writing. The following excerpts are from Craig's journal:

Surprising . . . that common denominators evolved among such different people. Surprising that people were so secure. . . . It may say a lot about how we function given a mutual support environment that we are genuine participants in.

Writing—I wrote earlier today about it. I really wonder if I used it to guide my way out of teaching (purposeful). . . . Paradoxical—one only needs to read to see how often my perceptions were tied to other things than the immediate circumstances. Black can be white. . . .

What happened to my diary? The essence of the answer lies in what happened to me. The end result is that I became very unhappy and bored. . . . I enjoyed the early writing immensely. It was creatively and intellectually stimulating and the cathartic effect of it was marvelous. Setting down for permanent record those many passing moments and thoughts was really rewarding. It was there to see for real. Ideas had been captured from the subconscious nooks of my brain, analyzed and brought to life. I was fascinated by how well I could write, just another of the things that made the diary a self-rewarding endeavor.

Much of the early writing lacks a reference point in time. Sure there are dates but many entries are thoughts from years past that recur from time to time. I wanted to get it all down. For years I had so much to say about education and now I had a safe and supportive forum to speak. I wrote voluminously while I had all this to say. Old thoughts and narrative accounts of daily events provided an abundance of materials.

But then the trouble started. When the time came when the only way to go was deeper analysis and showdowns with the big question I choked.

First I didn't want to deal with them. I ask kids "why" questions but am reluctant to answer them about myself. . . .

As Craig notes, the diary can be a significant and rewarding way to talk about practice (I use the word *practice* to include the broad range of responsibilities and interactions involved in being a teacher in addition to the more specific acts of teaching). But it is here, at the point where Craig begins to find discomfort in reflection, that the potential significance of writing as a tool for teaching and professional development begins to emerge—that the distinctions between writing a personal diary and keeping a personal-professional journal become more clear.

The diary function allows for spontaneous ideas and narrative accounts of daily events, but the journal extends beyond these to include deliberative thought and analysis related to practice. (We will look more closely at the distinctions between these two types of personal documents in chapter 2.) In some ways the writing is comparable to a relaxed chat with a colleague over coffee in the teachers' lounge. But while constructive analysis for change can happen in the diary or in the teachers' lounge, it usually doesn't. Airing a problem in this manner can be likened to a first draft. Although it can lead to planning and action, it more frequently gets lost in a myriad of other topics, other concerns. For analysis and constructive change to occur, the journal should provide sustained momentum.

CHAPTER 2

Logs, Diaries, and Journals

The one absolute requirement for me to write
. . . is to be awake.

Isaac Asimov

By keeping a personal-professional journal you are both the learner and the one who teaches. You can chronicle events as they happen, have a dialogue with facts and interpretations, and learn from experience. A journal can be used for analysis and introspection. Reviewed over time, it becomes a dialogue with yourself. Patterns and relationships emerge. Distance makes new perspectives possible; deeper levels of insight can form. Analyzing his journal, Jerry finds that "My biases shine!" He feels humility and exhilaration as he ponders his experience: "Did I really do all that?"

LOGS, DIARIES, AND JOURNALS

Personal documents or, as some people describe them, private chronicles are as old as written language. History is in many ways a journal—someone's impressions, thoughts, ideas, and not as obviously, his or her interpretations of events. There are many types of personal documents: letters, pictures, film, logs, diaries, and journals. Books, both historical and literary, are often reconstructed accounts from such documents.

Most people who write about diaries and journals do not make a distinction between the two; in common usage the words are often used interchangeably. Fothergill (1974) refers to the "personal diary . . . the diary whose prime subject is the life of the writer, valued for its own sake" (3). He writes that " 'Diary' means what you think it means; moreover its usage appears to be indistinguishable from that of 'journal' " (3).

As Mallon (1984) puts it, the two ". . . are in fact hopelessly muddled" (1). Both *diary* and *journal* stem from a Latin root that means "day." For our purposes, however, it is useful to distinguish among logs, diaries, and journals. Each calls for different methods of writing and record keeping.

Logs

According to the *Merriam-Webster Dictionary*, a *log* is, among other things, a "daily record of a ship's progress; also: a regularly kept record of performance." Log books are the official records of a ship's voyage, containing information on course, speeds, distances, and other navigational details, as entered by the watch officer. Logs, when defined as regularly kept records of performance, are also used by scientists, writers, teachers, and others to record selected information. Just as the ship's log is a description of conditions and happenings, other types of logs are used to record facts pertaining to specific occurrences.

Many teachers find it useful to keep logs of children's behavior and progress in school. In this way, patterns of behavior and learning styles can be identified. When a teacher needs information on a student who presents unusual challenges or has special problems, a log can be useful in data collection, analysis, and planning.

For example, Joy, a soft-spoken eight-year-old, had to work diligently to complete school assignments. Though timid and noninitiating in her interactions with most other children, she had several friends with whom she worked and played. In the middle of the year, Barb, my co-teacher, and I noticed that Joy had begun behaving strangely at times: she seemed irritable and inattentive, and she refused to play with other children. By midday she often appeared to be tired. On other days she was the Joy we had known before.

We began to log her behavior each time it deviated from "normal." After three weeks we realized that her behavior seemed to be day-related—specifically, Thursday-related. We discovered that on Wednesday and Friday nights Joy went to church with her parents and baby brother. While her parents attended meetings, she sat in a room in the church basement and cared for her brother. By 11:30, when the family arrived home, Joy had been up for three hours past her normal bedtime. While the story is more complicated than this (discussion with Joy's parents uncovered several other problems), by keeping a log of this child's actions we were able to unravel the mystery of her behavior.

Teachers also use logs to document students' social interactions at school and to record academic progress. One teacher, for example, has her students keep logs of the books that they read over a term. From these she identifies what each student reads, their progress in levels of difficulty, and also the variety of books they select.

Many of us find that logs are valuable aids to planning. Lesson plan books function as logs for recording what we plan to do—whether it be teaching or administration. If we return to these plans and record what actually transpired, we can log our progress, curricular development, or topics discussed, which we can use for subsequent evaluation and planning.

One group of teachers found it useful to keep time budget logs of interactions with persons other than their students during several teaching days. Figure 2–1 is one kindergarten teacher's daily time log. When he analyzed the logs for several days he was surprised to find the number of interruptions to his teaching, the range of topics in the interactions, with whom he spoke, and the day-to-day variations. Such logs might also be useful in discussion across classrooms, grade levels, even districts. Are there more frequent interruptions in elementary school classrooms than in high school? What happens to the class—to teaching and learning— as a result? Does it depend on the type of interruption? For example, if Martha, a high school math teacher, ducks into the hallway to chat with the teacher next door, is her class more relaxed and productive because she has had relief from some of the tensions of teaching?

Researchers use logs to record changes over time. In the Grant study, for example (one of the longest and most comprehensive studies of adult development yet reported), researchers kept logs on more than two hundred men over a thirty-year period. They recorded information relating to several aspects of the subjects' lives, including career, social health, psychological health, physical health, childhood environment, marital happiness, and methods of adapting to life. In a book reporting on ninety-five of the men, Vaillant (1977) uses a nautical metaphor to highlight the importance of keeping records over time, not as answers in themselves, but as indispensable data for analysis.

> [T]he study of lifetimes is comparable to the study of celestial navigation. Neither a sextant nor celestial map can predict where we should go; but both are invaluable in letting us identify where we are. Both in my own life and in my clinical work with patients, I have found that the lives of the Grant Study men provide navigational charts of greatest utility. (373)

In summary, a log is a factual account maintained over time. Usually there is a standardized format for recording so that data are objective. Recording is rule-governed. Analysis and interpretation follow the col-

FIGURE 2–1
Time Log

Date 4-13-82

Time	Dura-tion	Who	What/Why	Where	Typical	Comments
8:30	2 min	1st Grade Teachrs	Making list of where balloon cards came from.	Their rooms	no	
8:40	1 min	1st Grade Teacher	Looking at map to locate towns where cards came from	My room	no	
8:40 - 10:30			Routine classroom proceedings			
10:30	30 Sec	1st Grade Teacher	Stopped to tell me Jason moved	Hall way	?	
TO 11:20			Routine class			
11:25 1:40	15 min		Eating lunch in lounge		Yes	
12:25	30 sec	Sec + 3 cd grade teacher	Teacher's mother is ill and wants to leave. Dale is gone. My decision	My room	No	Call a sub
2:20	2 min	Parent Tutor	Giving instructions for working w/ kid	"	Yes	
2:25	2 min	Another parent tutor	"	"	"	
2:55	10 sec	Tutors	Checking in	Room	"	

lection of log data. Over time, patterns of behavior or events can become evident.

Diaries

The *Merriam-Webster Dictionary* defines a *diary* as "a daily record, esp. of personal experiences and observations; also: a book for keeping such private notes and records." Whereas logs are limited in topic and highly structured, diaries are filled with everything. Most often they are spontaneous accounts of whatever strikes the author's fancy or stirs a discord strong enough to write about. It is the one place where a person can present a point of view unencumbered by dissenting opinions: "As I write, there arises somewhere in my head that queer and very pleasant sense of something which I want to write; my own point of view" (Virginia Woolf, April 8, 1921). Were we each to have someone to relate our stories to as they evolve, in all the stark and raw reality we feel, diaries might not be so appealing. They would, however, still have the advantage of enabling us to return to them, and to think over their contents.

Diaries provide a format for authors to "let it all out" without concern for how others will interpret and judge their thoughts and feelings. When we write openly, the intensity of our reactions can be a surprise; we find ourselves feeling the same emotions all over again. We wonder, as Craig did when he wrote the following excerpt, "Did I really feel that strongly about that?" At the end of one very frustrating day he wrote:

> Justine, Justine, Justine. I'd rather drink prune juice for a week than talk any more about that child.
>
> The big mystery about the kid remains and the parents offered their usual aura of important but withheld information. I said I was out of suggestions and we were out of time after two years. . . .
>
> These people lie! They tell me she can do the work at home and is sociable with the neighborhood kids. Then I hear from the speech therapist this tale of woe poured out by Mrs. Justine about how uncooperative Justine is at home and she won't do any school type work at all. To hell with it . . . I really don't care what happens to this kid now. I can barely stand the sight of her and my only remaining concern is that I meet her little brother without prejudice next year.
>
> That's strong stuff Craig. It's sad that it's so genuine.

Having a benign friend, one who listens and reflects back our words, is a rare opportunity. "Dear Diary" is such a friend. Virginia Woolf referred to her diary as a "kindly blankfaced old confidante"; to Anne Frank (1952) it was a friend with whom to have a conversation:

> In order to enhance in my mind's eye the picture of the friend for whom I have waited so long, I don't want to set down a series of bald facts in a diary like most people do, but I want this diary itself to be my friend, and I shall call my friend Kitty. (13)

At 86 years of age, Florida Scott-Maxwell (1968) found her notebook to be

> my dear companion, or my undoing. I put down my sweeping opinions, prejudices, limitations, and just here the book fails me

for it makes no comment. It is even my wailing wall, and when I play that grim, comforting game of noting how wrong everyone else is, my book is silent, and I listen to the stillness, and I learn. (8)

The purpose, style and type of writing, as well as the demeanor of the writer, is usually quite different in diaries than it is in logs. The way events are described is dictated by the writer's thoughts and feelings about them: factual information is included in a way that supports the writer's perspective at the time. There is less concern for objectivity and more attention to the way experiences feel. In spontaneous writing, importance is placed on freshness of perception, of capturing impressions lived, rather than on careful documentation and thoughtful reconstruction of events and circumstances. Depending on the purposes and moods of the writer, diary entries can be factual, creative, emotional, thoughtful, deliberate, or impressionistic.

In general, diaries are open-ended: anything that can be verbalized can be included. At times, the writer has a specific topic in mind to write about; at other times, thoughts flow onto the page unrestrictedly. The degree of structure framing the writing depends entirely on the writer. Diary entries can be as structured as those of a log, though log entries are rarely as free-flowing as diary entries.

Because diary writing is interpretive, descriptive in multiple dimensions, sometimes factual, and often all of these, it is difficult to analyze. Few writers return to their diaries with systematic analysis in mind. It isn't easy to separate thoughts from feelings or facts and to disassociate oneself from the writing. Log writers usually don't have these problems, since logs are often kept with other readers in mind and without the incrimination of opinion. But most of us would cringe at the thought of others reading everything we write in our diaries! Whereas it would be a rare person who would care to read someone else's log, there are many people who would relish reading another's diary. As Evelyn Waugh (1976) put it, "Nobody wants to read other people's reflections on life and religion and politics, but the routine of their day, properly recorded, is always interesting" (as cited in Mallon 1984, frontispiece)—especially if presented with candor.

These apparent constraints to analysis—the open nature of entries and the personal interpretations we lend to them—are also sources of the diary's potential strengths and uses. For example, who helps us absorb those aspects of our teaching days that we must? Who listens with a quiet heart and without judgment to our thoughts and feelings about what we see and hear, what we do, and what happens to us as teachers? How do we remove ourselves for stretches from the busyness of teaching? Recording in our diaries stills the motion of doing and turns us to pondering on paper, while at the same time capturing some of the action of teaching for reflection.

Journals

Merriam-Webster's defines the *journal* as a "service book containing the day of hours . . . 1: a brief account of daily events   2: a record of proceedings (as of a legislative body)   3: a periodical (as a newspaper) dealing esp. with current events."

Journal writing can include the structured, descriptive, and objective notes of the log and the free-flowing, impressionistic meanderings of the diary. It is more difficult and demanding to keep; it is more complex. Its advantages are also greater: it combines purposes and extends into other uses. The contents of a journal are more comprehensive than those of either a log or a diary. It is a reconstruction of experience and, like the diary, has both objective and subjective dimensions, but unlike most diaries, the writer is (or becomes) aware of the difference. The journal as a "service book" is implicitly a book someone returns to. It serves purposes beyond recording events and pouring out thoughts and feelings. The term has ties to the newspaper trade and suggests a brief account rather than a description of everything the author finds of interest. Like the diary, the journal is a place to "let it all out." But the journal is also a place for making sense of what *is* out, whether for a newspaper article or the writer's private understanding. The journal is a working document.

In a journal, the writer can carry on a dialogue with various dimensions of experience. What happened? What are the facts? What was my role? What feelings surrounded the event? What did I feel about what I did? Why? What was the setting? The steps involved? And later, what were the important elements? What preceded the event? Followed it? What might I be aware of if such a situation recurs? This dialogue, between objective and subjective views, between description and interpretation, allows the writer to become more accepting and less judgmental as a flow of events takes form. Actions interconnect and take on new meaning.

A journal, as it is addressed in this book, is a tool for personal and professional growth, "an instrument for recording and then evaluating . . . a means to reflection . . . its essence is subtle movement and change . . . a collage of life in motion . . ." (Progoff 1975, 16–21). It includes log and diary writing but it is not time-bound. Parts of the journal can be sequential in time, but much is not. The writer often documents events as they occur (daily, weekly) but also ranges unfettered through time to explore and connect topics and questions. Themes and patterns emerge through analysis and interpretation.

A *research journal* (or section of a journal) is a tool for focusing on a specific topic or challenge. Many researchers keep detailed journals, documenting their ideas and working hypotheses and collecting evidence (data) along the way. They use the journal as documentation for both formative and summative analysis and evaluation. For formative evaluation the implicit question is "What is happening now?" The researcher records events as they occur, or as soon after as possible. Often, for example, the researcher makes jottings, or brief notes, so that potentially valuable information isn't lost. This helps in reconstructing circumstances and events when time to write is available. In summative evaluation, the researcher asks "What happened?" In addition to analyzing data, the researcher often re-searches to fill in information that was omitted or now seems appropriate to augment the original data.

A research journal can be used to keep comprehensive, descriptive documentation, to record facts, procedures, and interactions (including verbal information), and to keep analytical and interpretive notes. Factual, analytical, and interpretive notes are classified as such, for they are used in the reconstruction of the subject of research from objective and subjective perspectives. The purposes of research as well as the procedures used will dictate the content and methods of writing in the research journal. In some studies (e.g., the Grant study, Vaillant 1977), fundamental research questions and categories for data collection are established before the study begins. Additional questions become important as the study evolves.

In the Teacher Reflections study, general research questions also were posed before the study began. These were altered as the study progressed; as information was collected and analyzed, new directions and questions emerged. "How do teachers help other teachers?" branched into "What happens when teachers write about and discuss their teaching and concerns on a weekly basis?", "What happens to teachers as they write reflectively about their lives as teachers?", and "Are there changes, or stages, or phases one goes through in keeping a journal over time? If so, what are they?" (See Appendix A.)

The research journal for the Teacher Reflections study began with open-ended entries. Classroom observations were recorded in a general way—with the researcher as a visitor to a new planet, not quite sure what everything means but intrigued by many details. Writing on the following topics filled pages of the observation section of my journal:

- Classroom time (when school began, length of lessons) and use of physical space (bulletin boards, what and where, seating arrangements).
- Interactions (teacher and students with whom, when, and why). These often included sketches (see Figure 2–2).

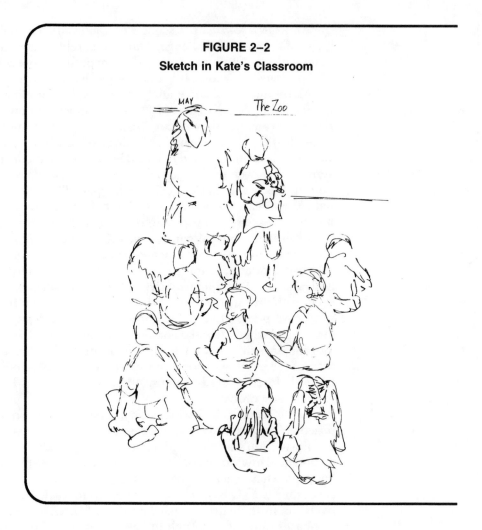

FIGURE 2–2
Sketch in Kate's Classroom

- General feelings (I feel at home here, students seem in slow motion, this class feels like Beethoven's *Fifth* sounds).
- Questions (Where do students who leave the room go? What are the teacher's thoughts and feelings about the texts used? Why did the teacher seem surprised at the student's response? Why did the students seem to hurry to finish the maps they so painstakingly worked on before lunch?).
- Events and circumstances surrounding the observations for both the teacher and me (The teacher had a difficult meeting with a parent yesterday afternoon; what will I do about my class tonight with a last-minute cancellation from the guest speaker?).

Later entries are more focused. As I analyzed what I saw and recorded in my journals, questions arose that guided subsequent observations. It was as if this teacher and this classroom were part of one big mystery. I asked myself, "What are the important elements? What relates to what?" The longer I observed, the more differentiated the information became.

Take Kate, for example. She is a kindergarten teacher in a small rural district and had been teaching for fifteen years in the same classroom. At the beginning of the school year, Kate noticed a change in her attitude and behavior from previous years. Each year, to acclimate the children to their first school, she invited six of them and their mothers to visit school for a few hours the week before the year began. This served three major purposes: Kate could observe the children with their mothers, slowly introduce the children to a major change in their lives (the primary purpose), and communicate with the mothers about school. In previous years Kate had been highly conscious of modeling appropriate behavior and the mothers' reactions to her as she took the children around the room and introduced them to materials and work and play areas. This year she was all but oblivious to the mothers until she finished talking with the children. Only then did she focus on the mothers and their questions. Reflecting on this, Kate found that "everything felt right." She wrote herself a large reminder in her journal, which she kept open on her desk: *the children come first*! She had concentrated on the children; she tried to understand how they might feel and perceive this big day. As she thought back to other first days, she realized that she had now gained a level of confidence that enabled her to focus attention outside herself. What she thought about and wrote about became her focus.

Our conversation about these changes led me to look differently at her teaching, to key my observations to different aspects of teaching. Not only did this discussion with Kate change the focus of my observations in Kate's room, it also influenced my observations in other classrooms. The concepts of maturation and experience in teaching were brought to the fore. Did other teachers have similar experiences? Would a younger or less experienced teacher have different concerns?

Some teachers keep research sections in their journals; others make no distinction between systematic inquiry and problem solving and other types of writing. In the example in Figure 2–3, taken from Jerry's journal, we find facts recorded on one side of the page and Jerry's reactions on the other. He decided to try this after rereading his journal and noticing how his interpretations sometimes mingled with facts and took on an unwarranted air of certainty (Figure 2–4). In Figure 2–3 he tries consciously to separate the two.

To summarize the distinctions among logs, diaries, and journals, the log is an objective record of information (pages read, attendance, activ-

FIGURE 2–3
Jerry's Journal Excerpt:
Log and Interpretation

79 A

101

Adam: Mr. Jensen, could you tell me how to spell igloo's.

Me: Sure Adam. (I spell it *write* for him on his card) What assignment are you working on?.

Adam: Assignment?

Me: Yes. (looking toward the board) Spelling, Phonics, language, Reading — which assignment?

Adam: Oh, I'm done with all of those things.

Me: "Are you writing a story then?"

Adam: Well, yes, and no, well yes, I guess I am. Well, going to.

Me: So, you've finished up and you are going to write a story.

Adam: Well, no, not exactly. I haven't finished my reading yet.

Perhaps I'm too *now so?* structured — rigid. I am concerned that Adam doesn't participate in a lot of the class room activities as I feel he should. It comes down to responsibility I suppose. I am responsible for what Aaron does in his second grade year of schooling and so far he has been very uncooperative. I need a sense of direction with him and we haven't found a common ground so far.

FIGURE 2–4

Jerry's Journal Excerpt:
Mingling Facts and Interpretation

My last notable challenge is Adam Copeland. Certainly not least though! In fact, had I rank ordered them he would have been 1st. He's a bright little boy and has few good social skills. He can do nice work but rarely does any. He can not express himself in an academic situation and rarely contributes to class room discussions. He finds humor in being reprimanded and generally doesn't care about social graces. He continually gurgles and grunts as his nose runs freely. He has on occasion burped as one would after having successfully guzzled a 16 oz. soda. Upon burping he grins as though it was an accomplishment and a major contribution to the class. He is a strange child and I'll be searching for ways to help him become social. I do not intend breaking his will and harnessing him as though he was—is—a wild animal. There is a wide range of acceptable (socially) behaviors. My intent is to help him gain just a few.

Karry talks too much. I think this will take care of itself when I find a good group for her to sit with.

with his pocket → Berl plays. Yesterday he tied himself in his seat. Sat up 4 crayons on end and began to push them forward as one would a control lever. Upon pushing the 4th and final one forward he jettisoned himself backwards and supplied the appropriate "blast off" sounds. He grinned with pride at being successful and gained quite a few looks from his peers. None were approving except of course Peggy

ities, lesson plans); the diary is a personal document in which the author can record log-type information but is primarily a book for expressing the author's thoughts, reactions, ideas, and feelings related to everyday experiences; and the journal is a document that includes both the objective data of the log and the personal interpretations and expressions of experience of the diary, but which moves beyond these to intentional personal and professional reflection, analysis, planning, and evaluation.

FURTHER REACHES

For most of us, there is a ubiquitous reader. Sometimes the reader is one of many selves, or dimensions of us. Virginia Woolf asks "Whom do I tell when I tell a blank page?" (August 5, 1929). Christina Baldwin (1977) comments on the self who writes the journal and on another self who reads it. We find ourselves writing with someone peering over our shoulder even when we do not wish consciously to share our writing with others. "Dear Diary" invades even our journals. Many of our entries are like letters. Sometimes we write to ourselves, sometimes to others. The self who experiences events records them for the self who might not remember them. The self in a muddle can write its piece and prevail upon another self who has the luxury of distance and age to help with interpretation. We capture our experiences to make sense of them. As Virginia Woolf noted, "The past is beautiful because one never realizes an emotion at the time. It expands later, and thus we don't have complete emotions about the present, only about the past . . ." (quoted in Mallon 1984, 33).

People keep diaries and journals for many reasons. Mallon (1984) organizes diary writers into seven types. He cites Pepys for accidentally setting an example as *chronicler*—of the everyday contents of his life and times. As the New Year began in 1660, so did the written story of Pepys. So regular a part of Pepys' life did writing become that while keeping a diary over a period of 3,438 days, he missed recording on only 11! Unlike the chroniclers, *travelers* leave a record of special circumstances: traveling to foreign lands, noting scenery, people, itineraries. Whether one is keeping a journal as an explorer (Lewis and Clark) or as a tourist (Aunt Dorothy's visit to Disneyland), the purpose is to have a record to return to.

One of the most prevalent types of journal is that kept by the *pilgrim*, a person who sets out to explore "Who am I?" Journal writing is used for personal growth and self-understanding; the author purposely undertakes an inner journey. Theoretically, for such persons the journal is therapeutic; it enables catharsis, integration, self-acceptance, and change. Thoreau, for example, used his journal to work toward enlightenment. The journal was a place where he could record thoughts and feelings while communing with nature. In 1841 he wrote, "My journal is that of me which would else spill over and run to waste, gleanings from the field which in action I reap." He seeks to "meet [myself] face to face sooner or later." For Thoreau the journey is solitary; friends do not understand his need to be alone, to "commit my thoughts to a diary even on my walks, instead of seeking to share them generously with a friend" (quoted in Mallon 1984, 77).

Ira Progoff (1975), a contemporary pilgrim, writes that "*the intensive journal* process [which he created] is offered as an instrument with a day-by-day method [or] means of private and personal discipline with which to develop our inner muscles" (15). In contrast to Thoreau's isolated solitude, Progoff points to the benefit of writing in the presence of others. "The presence of other persons . . . each exploring the individuality of his own life history, builds an atmosphere that supports and strengthens his inward work . . ." (11).

Artists, creators, and inventors keep journals to sketch their ideas, to record readings, and to react to ideas. Poets, novelists, painters, architects, composers, and scientists note on paper the birth of their creations. These are the *creators*. Another group of journal and diary writers are called the *apologists*. These people "wish to explain, to justify, to plead a case before history . . . not only to make history but to write it as well— or at least to get their versions on record . . ." (Mallon 1984, 167). Politicians (Richard Nixon, for example) and historians are prominent in this group.

The *confessor* is the person who writes to acknowledge sins and to expiate them.

> [T]he diary had become, by the late nineteenth century, more typically the place in which they could savor them [sins]. . . . By unburdening one's soul on paper, one could have one's sins and remember them too. Confession was still good for the soul but now it could be a positive delight to the eyes as well. (Mallon 1984, 208–9)

The Diary of Anne Frank, though written by an adolescent, is of a different sort. Anne, like other *prisoners*, figurative and literal, uses her diary to react to daily life in ways that she is not able to in a restrictive outer world. It becomes her interaction with outside: her emotions, thoughts, feelings, reactions—her intense responses to life. "Those violent outbursts on paper were only giving vent to anger which in normal life could have been worked off by stamping my feet a couple of times in a locked room, or calling Mummy names behind her back" (Frank 1952, 115).

Most of us write in our journals in several or all of the these ways. We use them to confess, to tell our side of the story, to cope with life, and to come to know ourselves better. We write in order to create and to mark our special experiences. We write in order to come to know our thoughts, to sort out thoughts and feelings, to plan, and to explore our problems. In doing so, writing promotes confidence in personal and professional spheres. It enables us to see and feel humanness, vulnerability, strength, and development.

It seems likely that if we explore the world within and the world outside, we will grow in understanding of both, and in our relationships. It is in balancing the journey that the journal can be of greatest help. While, as Joseph Conrad said, "We can never cease to be ourselves" (quoted in Mallon 1984, xvii), we can become overly critical or optimistic and distort our picture of ourselves if we do not also explore the larger contexts within which we live. In expanding our communication with and awareness of others we gain perspective on ourselves, and through looking deeply into ourselves we learn about the world. Through a dialogue of introspection and expansion, integration and growth are possible. For introspection and expansion we can read of other persons' journeys; "one cannot read a diary and feel unacquainted with its writer. No form of expression more emphatically embodies the expressor: diaries are the flesh made word" (Mallon 1984, xvii).

SECTION II

Portraits of Teacher Journal Writers

I'll be hanged if I am not in a humor for shedding ink tonight—feel as if I could scribble, scribble, scribble to the extent of a quart bottle full.

George Templeton Strong

Just a few lines to tell you that this story is all about myself—for no other purpose do I write it. . . . There is no plot in this story, because there has been none in my life or in any other life which has come under my notice. I am one of a class, the individuals of which have not time for plots in their life, but have all they can do to get their work done without indulging in such a luxury.

Miles Franklin

I think it is true that one gains a certain hold on sausage and haddock by writing them down.

Virginia Woolf

Some people keep journals because they enjoy the act of writing, of scribbling across the page, recording their recollections and fantasies. Others want indelibly to etch their lives into history. Still others write to understand themselves and their circumstances—love, work, children, and haddock.

Anne Frank found many reasons to write. Florida Scott-Maxwell began posing questions to herself in her sketchbook, which then became her notebook. Virginia Woolf found that diary writing brought her closer to reality and helped her to develop ideas for professional writing. Sylvia Ashton-Warner wrote about her personal and professional worlds living and teaching in small Maori communities in New Zealand.

Unlike these published journal writers, the teacher-journalists presented here did not decide on their own to write journals. They were asked to. As with other journal writers, they found many different reasons to write, and their stories developed in individual ways. They found that their writing changed over time and that reflective writing aided in exploring different facets of teaching and professional development. What began as "reflective writing for the researcher" became "reflective writing for learning about teaching and me."

Near the end of her journal Carole wrote of her renewed commitment to her profession. She, as the others, found teaching to be more complicated and self-involving than she had realized before she began to write about it. Only one of the teachers, Jerry, wrote every so often "just for the pleasure of it" before starting the journal. "But how can I write about teaching? Teaching is like breathing, you just do it!" he said.

"Try writing about a few events or experiences, feelings, or thoughts that occur to you as you reflect on the day," I suggested. After a few months of writing, he felt differently: "I can't believe I never thought about some of these things before!" Jerry was reflecting on the meaning of teaching.

These teachers charted new professional territory when they agreed to keep track of themselves for a year. Though we couldn't have expressed it at the time, journal writing became a way for us to explore our own theories of teaching and professional development. Our theories were implicit—and sometimes explicit—in our writing. By writing about teaching, new thoughts were stimulated. By talking with others, our theories and questions were challenged and developed. By returning to the journal, we could explore our ideas from different perspectives and see how they developed. We wrote about teaching in a time of "the hurried child" (Elkind 1983), when teacher isolation (Lortie 1975) was a felt reality, and when the curriculum was becoming more standardized and testing an increasingly influential aspect of teaching and evaluation. The word *reflection* was relatively new in education (Schön's *Reflective Practitioner* wasn't to appear until 1983), and the need to reflect with other teachers about these and other concerns was reason enough to agree to think on paper about them.

CHAPTER 3

Judy

Writing became a *way of thinking.*

I would play school and use the wall as my "pretend blackboard." I can remember studying for tests by being the teacher and lecturing "my students"! My mother's a school nurse and I can remember going to school functions and hearing people say, "Are you going to be a nurse like your mother?" How I hated that question. I hated hospitals and anything to do with them. My mother's reply was "No, she's going to be a teacher!" I honestly don't remember if she said that because that's what I wanted to be or because that's what she wanted me to be.

. . . [W]hen I began to teach people would say, "Oh, you get the summers off. What a good reason to teach." I was shocked because I had never thought about the summer. . . .

My grandmother was a teacher in a one-room schoolhouse. We used to compare notes and when she'd come for a visit we'd go to school. I'd show her my room and we'd discuss how things had changed. . . .

[T]eaching has always been a part of my life. I was even picked when I was in sixth grade to go to lower grades and teach when teachers had to leave for one reason or another and I received the FTA (Future Teachers of America) scholarship. . . .

At 31, Judy was in her tenth year of teaching at the primary level in a medium-sized suburban community. She and her husband Kurt were the parents of a two-year-old daughter. Kurt, a manager in business, had difficulty understanding why Judy spent so much time on schoolwork. And he wasn't much interested in discussing her teaching day with her. At school she lamented what little opportunity she had to engage in meaningful professional development activity: "Why isn't our in-service relevant?" "Why can't our lounge talk be deeper? More collegial?" "Why aren't we teachers supported professionally, commensurate with our responsibilities?" When the Teacher Reflections project began, Judy eagerly anticipated meeting with other teachers each week for seminars. Writing was, however, another matter, one she faced with trepidation. "What do I write about?" "When do I write?"

Judy began by writing about what she perceived to be her strengths and weaknesses as a teacher: "I have good rapport with my kids. . . . Sometimes I give one chance too many. . . . I hear myself saying 'this is your last chance.' . . ." Then, she wrote about individual children: "Tom seems to be somewhat hyper. . . ." She wrote of daily events in her classroom and school, of frustrations, and of things she noticed about her thinking. After two weeks of writing she noticed patterns and themes.

> Wed. 3/4
> . . . Very interesting—on way to school thought about things I needed to get done. There was nothing in those thoughts about the kids. It was all completing bulletin boards, grading papers & getting everything for averaging grades. . . .
>
> Thurs. 3/5
> Well here it is. Lesson plan day. It seems everyday I have so much paperwork that must be completed. I'm seeing a pattern here. Paperwork vs child time. . . . Tom was extremely quiet all morning. . . .

In many respects, Judy's early journal writing resembles that of many other teachers' later journal writing. It was casual. She wrote immediately of her apprehensions about writing and about being a project participant. She wrote of satisfactions, frustrations, colleagues, her teaching, and of seminar sessions and comments from other teachers. Almost immediately her journal became a place to talk to herself. In the first of two journal excerpts, Judy writes of "our evening together," which followed her first night of participation in the seminar. The second excerpt is written a month later and exemplifies her deepening insights about writing as well as her ongoing concerns about it.

> This was a very rewarding yet frustrating evening. . . . I had a variety of feelings.
> [It] will be good for me. I think it'll motivate me to become a better teacher and to try to do new things. I really like Kate's program of involving parents. There's some topnotch teachers here.
> That leads me to my own feelings of inadequacy. I feel like I'm out of my league. Yet, Mary Lou wouldn't have chosen me if she felt that I couldn't fit in. . . . This is something I'm going to have to deal with. It's known as an inferiority complex.

It was real interesting. Marcy Chapman is our ex assistant superintendent's wife . . . when we were sitting and brainstorming and she said teacher strikes . . . I immediately felt threatened (We've been through a strike . . .).

Why is it that as a teacher I feel threatened by the administration? I know my feelings are pretty common. It's really sad because we should be working together for the good of the children instead of having threatening feelings. There may be times that I'll just sit quietly because I won't feel comfortable sharing. But I will sit and write my feelings. . . .

Afterthought—I sure hope I'm expressing myself adequately. This is one area I can improve upon.

A month later:

Note the rambling [writing] this time, but this is how my mind's working today. There are a lot of generalities I need to get out of the way for me. Then I think I can get down to some real basics. It's like preparing a garden. First the earth has to be tilled—then the planting can begin. WOW! That makes no sense at all. Only I know that by getting these things out of the way I can get down to another level of thinking and hopefully writing. I wonder as I read this back how this is going to sound. . . .

A few days after:

I'm finding that it is very difficult for me to put down exactly what I want to say or to find the words to do it. I wonder if writing will ever become as easy as my talking? Writing is easier this time but I'm aware that expressing myself is difficult.

Throughout her diary Judy continues to comment on her difficulty with writing and especially in forming a "writing habit," of finding time and a quiet place to reflect. She usually wrote at home at night, but also sometimes during discretionary time (art, music, lunch, recess) at school.

Judy found writing to be cathartic: "Just writing makes me feel better!" She found that she could think on paper and through problems and dilemmas. The more she wrote, the more she could discern patterns in her behavior and intentions as well as in the children's. She found that she was able to move to a deeper, more introspective level more quickly the more she wrote. She also felt discomfort when she "went in too deeply," and intentionally returned to a "surface level" until she was ready to return to "deeper" concerns or introspection.

Writing for Judy often became a "contract with myself." When she discovered something through writing, she felt compelled to do something about it, to act on what she found out rather than to "push it aside like I would have done before." In August, after rereading her spring journal, she wrote the following:

> I've seen my writing evolve. At first it was very difficult and at times it still is. I find that I have two levels of writing. A surface level—telling about days' events, etc. On a second level—here my writing tends to get sloppy because I try to put down my inner thoughts and feelings before they escape. . . . [T]his is a more painful writing because I must confront myself. . . . [It has] made me see things I don't think I would ever have.

A few weeks later, planning for the school year, Judy writes,

> I've realized something about myself thru writing. Not realized it but have had to face it. I'm a great one for setting goals, but I usually come short of completing them *completely*. I stop somewhat between midway and the end. So this year instead of setting 10 goals I will set three that I feel I can obtain.

In September, after a seminar session, Judy continues to write about writing and its consequences.

> Thursday we were talking about how and when we write. . . . If someone were to ask me if writing and our informal sessions are a necessity, I'd have to give a definite "yes." But if they were to ask me if I've developed the self-discipline for my writing, I'd have to say "no." I don't feel comfortable reading my writing. There's nothing fancy to it. . . . But perhaps from all this I'll be able to develop my own style. . . .
> . . . I'm finding that I'm speaking out more to Mr. W. [her principal] about things I see and feel. I'd like him to be a more "personable" person to my kids and also to the staff. I don't feel threatened by his administrative position and I don't get upset by some of his "ideas and edicts." He is worried about his position. I guess what I'm saying is I see him more as a person . . . I'm finding that I'm becoming more sensitive to others.
> . . . I'm finding it much more difficult to find time to write this year though I enjoy writing more and find it more gratifying. Part is a bigger house—part is that Sherry [daughter] is at a

> sharing stage and she needs me there more. . . . But I do need to discipline myself to find that time. . . .
>
> Also, I see patterns in my writing and patterns in my thinking—philosophy. . . . It is rewarding. And as I said today, I can't believe I've written all this. I've gotten to my lower level. . . .

And, a few days later,

> Here it is the end of September—beginning of October and our group is finding that . . . some are having difficulty writing because they're—we're—getting to that lower level—very interesting. Where do we go or what do we do with ourselves or our writing when we get to that lower level? I don't think we can become too self-evaluative or too critical because then it gets to the point that we "lose sight of the forest for the hedge." We lose ourselves in all the self evaluativeness—we begin to get very frustrated, unhappy and discontented with ourselves because we only see things that we could improve upon.

Judy also became more confident of her ability to face and learn from her "mistakes." She saw, for example, how her feelings about (and affection toward) children influenced her teaching decisions.

> I had Tod last year. He's now in third grade with Sherry [his teacher] and comes to me for reading. He fits in well with my class. Why didn't I retain him? Why did I send him on? . . . There are no excuses, especially when we're discussing a child's life. But I wonder why I made the wrong decision. . . . Thinking back, I can remember . . . Tod and David "worked" together. They were on the same level. I retained David and not Tod. I wrote much more about David and Albert. I really should have written more about Tod. I've really concluded that if I devoted as much time (written time) to him as I did to the other two boys—he'd be with second grade. . . . They're saying (principal and other teacher) that because he was LD [learning disabled] we were hoping for more tutoring time—that's why he went on. But that's only an excuse. Actually, I've been using it too because I feel as if I need something to fall back on, when what I really need is to be honest. . . .

Ten days later, Judy writes of a meeting with Tod's parents, the principal, Sherry, the school psychologist, the learning disabilities tutor and teacher:

I had seen Mom last week and apologized. But after the meeting I talked to both and told them that I was sorry I had to have them go through this and that I should have foreseen this. That I really like Tod and perhaps some of my feelings entered into my decision. . . . I hadn't been objective. Tod hasn't been to school this week. He's had a high temperature. Today he left for school but went back home. He's having trouble coping. Not coming back to me, but what older kids will say. . . . Naturally this conference was very upsetting. I cried half way home and decided what's done is done. I learned. . . .

As she wrote about some of her frustrations, she began to identify still other concerns she hadn't been aware of. These included, for example, providing support for parents:

Connie's mom and I had a long talk. She's going through a divorce. I think she's handling it remarkably well. She has four girls and works nights and I think it helped her to be able to talk. It's interesting, but many times parents need to talk about themselves. . . . [A]fter all, this affects their kids' lives too. . . .

She also touches on puzzles and paradoxes that face those in her vocation:

If kids could only *voice* in words other than behavior some of their feelings. For that matter if adults would only do the same —then again how many teachers, peers, etc. would *really* listen and try to help?

Summing up her thoughts on reflective writing at the end of the project, Judy wrote:

Writing. A chance to know myself. Yes. I know myself, after all I live with myself, but this was a chance to sit down and actually confront myself. Good and bad. Self-help: I made promises in . . . writing that I had to keep—levels of writing became a *way of thinking*. I've begun to think in terms of how I'd write about this. . . . An author—for no one else but myself. . . . Analyzing [writing] helped me to see solutions to problems—Tod [for example].

. . . As I look at children, I try to really "see" them, their daily lives, what affects them. . . .

. . . I'm a better teacher . . . more confident . . . able to handle stress better. . . . I've come to know myself better. I've been able to admit things . . . dealt with them and moved on.

I've realized that others feel and experience many of the things that I do. This is comforting. Many times I thought I was the only one out there feeling *inadequate*, ill prepared.

I want to be better. I want to give that extra push. It's easier for me to admit to my feelings and express them openly.

CHAPTER 4

Carole

The writing itself was very beneficial to me personally because it made me look at my teaching philosophy and how I was dealing with students, parents, and administrators. . . . I also learned that teaching is so much a part of my life in and outside of school. . . . *I've learned to appreciate "ME."*

Carole was born in a large Midwestern city in 1951. The middle child in a family of nine, she and her older sisters took responsibility for younger siblings while their mother worked as a domestic to support the family. "Carole will be the teacher in this family," her mother frequently reminded them.

Like many of her friends, Carole was assisted in her education by the federally funded Follow-Through Program for promising children from low-income families. At Bonnard Drew, a small nearby liberal arts college, she found coursework difficult, but with help from Follow-Through in developing study skills, she graduated and became "the teacher in this family."

Having taught at the primary level in two inner-city schools in Chillton (her home town), Carole, together with her new husband John, moved to Rothville, a small college town about an hour's drive away, where she accepted a first-grade teaching position. As the only black teacher, she often feels lonely, though "people are friendly."

There are some days when being Black is too difficult in a building that is all white. I feel an emptiness that I did not feel when I did teach in a building where the staff was integrated. . . .

It makes me think about my first year of teaching here. That year was quite an experience. First of all it was difficult for me because here I was coming from a system that had an integrated staff to one where everything was lily white. Being Black made me stick out like a sore thumb. At my first meeting with the principal, I was informed that there had been another Black teacher in the building a couple of years ago who was "hard-headed." This teacher (according to the principal) did not want to socialize with the other members of the staff and did not eat lunch with them. Because of her "hard-headedness" my new principal had her fired. I don't know if there is any truth to this story or not, I asked no one. My first impression of my new principal was "who the hell does he think he is?" I was also thinking to myself that I had the freedom to choose to eat with whomever I please and to socialize with whomever I please. But being new and somewhat afraid I decided that I had better be a good girl and not cause any waves. I'm sure that the fact that I was the only Black person in the building was already enough commotion. As I began to meet the other members of the staff I became more relaxed. Some of the teachers went out of their way to make me feel comfortable, others showed their ignorance of Black people and their culture, while others treated me as if I were inferior to them. This was not a new experience for me because these same reactions had been displayed during my college years at a predominantly white college. . . .

For many of the students I've worked with I have been as close to a Black person as they have ever come. It's amazing their inquisitiveness about my being different from them. I am happy to be able to answer some of their deep dark mysteries about Black folks and to answer them truthfully. . . . Having been born and raised in a totally Black environment has made my adjustment to an all white environment difficult but necessary.

Carole was in her ninth year of teaching when she became a participant in the Teacher Reflections project. She began writing by noting topics as they occurred to her and expanding on them later. Her writing style is straightforward and fairly formal, not unlike her speech. The following excerpt is taken from an early journal entry. The first two sentences are jottings that she later expands on in the paragraph below them.

Sent another note to Mrs. Fabberhurst.
Won't get a reply.

Nothing is more upsetting than parents that won't take the time to come to school for a conference. I have written so many notes to this parent asking her to come to school. . . . She doesn't even acknowledge that she received the notes. Her phone is disconnected . . . I sent a letter. . . . Again no reply. I guess I'll keep trying while her daughter continues to suffer. . . . I don't even know what the lady looks like.

Carole, like Judy, found writing to be cathartic. She unleashed on paper "many of the frustrations that had accumulated during my first eight years of teaching." She was surprised by her complaints, not realizing, she said, that she had kept them inside.

When I first began writing, I cited mainly those things about teaching that were not to my satisfaction. When I look back . . . I was very disenchanted about where I was as a teacher and my enthusiasm as a teacher. I had thought many times about leaving this profession . . . just to get a break from the many demands that teachers receive from students, administrators, parents and the community.

Recording her frustrations and sharing some of them with colleagues seemed to allow Carole to focus on teaching. She wrote of dilemmas and recorded thoughts and questions as she learned about teaching. She focused on reading and language arts and discovered that this had been a source of frustration.

Our building is fortunate in having a reading consultant. Her job is a mystery to me. She does not work with the children. She passes out the reading tests to the teachers, asks each teacher what page each child is on, hogs the reading materials and tells you what reading approach will be best for a child she had never worked with.

I guess I expected her to give individual help to those students needing remedial reading.

A new reading series had been adopted, and Carole and her colleagues had difficulty mastering the more complex and comprehensive program. Shortly before report-card time, reading tests were administered, followed by orders from the reading consultant that children were to be graded based on standardized scores on the test. "But I could have moved the children along faster had I known before it would determine their grades," lamented Carole. She wrote about the series and her observations of the children regarding reading and language arts. "What is reading to the children?" she wondered. So, she conducted a survey.

Today I took a survey about reading in my class. I wanted to know my students' thoughts about the purpose of reading. Following are [examples from] the questions and answers.

1. What do people do when they read? (Sit down; they look with their eyes; they enjoy themselves; they think.)
2. What do you have to do to learn to read? (Practice; look at the word; go to church and read the Bible; start with the easy books and go to the hard books.)
3. Why do people read? (It wouldn't be fun if when you grow up you can't read; to enjoy theirselves; so if their friends give them a letter they'll know how to read it.)
4. How can you tell you're a good reader? (You can read fast; you know your *b*'s from your *d*'s; when you don't make many mistakes; 'cause you read with expression; if you can read four books a day.)

Carole also studied math. She found that "lots of times they are able to do the work correctly but very seldom do they truly understand the process they are using." At the end of the year "they remembered vividly the times we had popcorn in math class and the time we used lollipops for counting . . . for next school year I should work on making math more fun. . . ." From these and other inquiries into curricular areas, Carole learned more about how the children thought and felt about aspects of the curriculum. She began to recognize the differences in perception between herself and the children, and among the children.

Carole's journal writing progressed from letting out her frustrations and documenting problems to more analytical, reflective, and focused writing about the students and her teaching. Frustrations were still evident, but the emphasis was on understanding and action rather than catharsis. In this, the first of several journal excerpts, she writes of the children's points of view:

The first day of school is always difficult for first graders. First of all in kindergarten they are almost in another world. Their little worlds extend from their room to the library, to the office, and to the playground. They have no idea where other rooms are located in the building.

Finding their new first grade classes can be quite frustrating. Some of them don't know who the teacher is, let alone where the room is. . . . They sadly come into the room wishing they could go home with their mom. It's so much safer to be with Mom when you don't know what to expect.

After about ½ hour of school first graders get very restless and begin to ask questions like "when is it time for lunch?" Boy it must be tough to adjust to sitting at a desk.

Carole tries to overcome problems in communication with the principal:

Lately, I've forced my principal to become a part of what's happening in my classroom by asking him to help me with activity. He likes to feel needed so I tell him that I need him in my room to do something with my students. . . . I've suggested to other teachers in my building that they also invite him in to get involved with their students.

In a later excerpt she reflects on the mutuality of influence in the classroom. She writes this after rereading her journal and thinking about it.

I Rub off on them—They rub off on me

If I'm polite—they're polite. If I am gloomy—they are gloomy. If they are excited—I am excited. If they show affection—I show affection. . . . We must be aware of how our positive attributes can rub off on the students we spend so much time with.

And, finally, she writes introspectively about her identification with the children. In the following example, she writes about a child who is abused—one of three children with serious family problems whom Carole frequently wrote about. Here, she rereads her journal and writes this addition:

How this problem affected my personal life.
I found it very difficult to separate the problem which Christy was having at home from my own personal life. I've been told that I should leave job problems on the job but oh how this problem lingered with me. . . . I kept trying to think of ways that I could possibly get Christy to tell about her home life and most of all I prayed for Christy and her parents.

In exploring questions about her teaching and the children, Carole learned other significant things about herself:

I began to appreciate myself and my contribution to education. I began to realize that it's not what others think of me as a teacher but how I view myself. Several times I wrote about the need for praise from administrators and I'm sure that this is a need that I have and many other teachers also share.

She found the "praise" she sought in her writing and she began to appreciate the subtle (and sometimes not so subtle) indications of growth and satisfaction from the children.

Carole feels that as a result of her involvement in the Teacher Reflections project she is more aware and sensitive to the needs of children, to the complexity of teaching, to herself as a person who teaches, and to the social and cultural environments within which she teaches. She wrote that through writing and collegial discussion she learned that "I have faults that I was not aware of . . . my attachment to my students affects my life outside of school and perhaps my relationship with my spouse"; that "there are certain things that I'll never be able to change"; and that many of "the same problems I've had difficulty dealing with are common to other teachers too." At the conclusion of the project Carole wrote about writing:

> The writing itself was difficult for me because of personal problems that I was trying to deal with and because of time. The writing was very beneficial to me personally because it made me look at my teaching philosophy and how I was dealing with students, parents, and administrators. I was forced through writing to take a look at myself. When I take a look at myself some things are hurting while others were pleasing. The writing was also beneficial to my students. . . .

Of greatest significance to Carole, she began to see the interactive nature of her home and school lives. According to Carole, the most influential factor in her school life was her personal problems at home: "Because things were lacking in my marriage, I devoted much time to my teaching and became very attached to my students." Having discovered the consuming role that teaching played in her life, Carole resolved to work towards a better balance.

CHAPTER 5

Jerry

How often do we question ourselves?

In 1951, when Jerry was three years old, his family moved from rural north central Tennessee to a farm in northeastern Ohio. He was the fourth child in a family of seven. Childhood was a carefree existence for Jerry, and he has especially fond memories of music:

> Music has always been part of my life. I enjoyed music as a child—my father and uncle played guitars and sang up a storm —also it was my favorite part of church. I began learning the guitar when I was 12 or 13 . . . I quit the first time because it was a lot like work—but regained my interest and still play a lot. . . .
>
> When I was a child time had little meaning. It meant seasons. Winter, spring, summer, fall. Sled riding and Mom's snow cream. Counting the days until the buds came out and we planned our garden out, planted and watched it grow. Then school is out, we play outside from daylight til dark, we work in the garden and have fun. Harvest begins, school begins and the time is just days between holidays and winter comes again. . . . High school was one big social event. I was an average student gradewise. The main goal of high school was to *graduate*! I had worked full time since my sophomore year as a service attendant and was satisfied with myself, my lot in life. I wasn't expected to do anything differently except perhaps to finally get a good job in a union shop. I worked for one year after graduation and was drafted. As an alternative to the Army, I joined the Air Force (one brother was an ex-marine, and another was in the Army in Viet Nam at that time).
>
> I was stationed in New Mexico for about 2½ years after my initial training as an Air Craft Maintenance Specialist. . . . I travelled a lot, over the States and Canada a few times. I met a lot of interesting people and learned a lot about myself.

The thought of going to college didn't occur to Jerry until he was 22 and had been in the Air Force for four years. College had until then been "something for other people."

> When I entered undergraduate school I had never really given any thought to "if I would finish or not." . . . [W]hen I got married in 1973 . . . I promised my wife I would complete the undergraduate degree program. . . . I was interested in becoming a social worker, working with juvenile delinquents. The more involved I became in the literature, the more I began to realize that, what I would like to do—what I *needed* to do—was work with kids *before* they got all screwed up. . . . I felt I could be more effective in preventative maintenance. . . . I decided I would become a teacher . . . to see if I could make an impact on their lives. . . . That is why I wanted to, and still want to, work with children.

Jerry has taught for six years in the primary grades at a kindergarten-through-grade-two school in an upper-middle-class bedroom community (population 14,000) bordering a middle-sized industrial city. The school system is well supported and has a fine reputation. Jerry feels quite comfortable working with the children, though their backgrounds are considerably different from his own. Along with his wife, a school psychologist, and their two children, he lives in a rural area thirty miles from where he teaches. His two closest colleagues also live outside the district.

Writing was not new to Jerry. He wrote poetry and occasionally kept diarylike notes, "just for me though, I enjoy writing." "Writing for me is a release," he notes. "But how can I write about teaching? Teaching is like breathing—you just do it!" "At the elementary level I find the essence of education and the essence of life essentially the same."

Jerry began by writing about individual children. He wrote journalistically, subjectively, and on several occasions autobiographically. His style of writing is casual, sometimes humorous, and often vivid, as he records his teaching day as only someone who has been there could do:

> **8:45** The entry bell rings and there they come. Sandy is usually first in the room since he is a walker. Sandy is a little loud and usually in a grand mood in the morning—probably because he is going to be away from home for 6 or so hours. He's a smart little boy—not exceptional—but smart. . . . (Sandy) "I know addition, subtract, multiply and divide, but I don't know ABLEGER yet. My brother is taking ABLEGER . . . and boy is my mom mad. She's yellin about why's he takin it so early." . . . Sandy's mother is always yelling about *something*. . . . Her first question to me in

the November parent conference was "What do the checks translate into grades?" (How many ways can you say THEY DON'T!) You see, Sandy's older brother is in the SOAR PROGRAM, the gifted class. I warned her about comparing siblings . . . but she and dad insist and it has really produced an ambivalent 2nd grader. When I have to talk to Sandy about an infraction or some concept clarification he cowers, mumbles and dreads a confrontation of any sort. . . .

8:50 Timothy—look at my new sneakers (I'm important!) I got a new pair of dress shoes too—they're at home—for my birthday—remember, it was last Friday. . . . 4 × 6 = 24—right? Yes Timothy that's right—very good—would you like to take lunch count this morning?

The room is half full by now—LUNCH COUNT !!?? I thought YOU (meaning me) were going to take lunch count to be able to say hello to all of us—a chorus from the class—

Well, yes, but I think Timothy will do a good job this morning, I'll sit here & say hello as you go by.

Kirk has a 145 I.Q. & is afraid of his shadow. Deena doesn't have a dad and I have been her male image and source since September [it is February]. Sometimes she hugs me & laughs *hysterically*— It's finally 9:05 and the class bell rings—time to begin our day— right?

Sandy—stroke for division.

Timothy—stroke for responsibility.

Deena—god only knows—Mom spent last 3 wks in Las Vegas—came home for a long weekend. She, Deena & brother at home went to Indiana to visit two older brothers in military school and Monday morning Deena was off to school & Mom to the Bahamas. . . .

9:10 I search for Diantha—she missed Thursday and Friday to visit her Dad since he's in town—visitation rights. . . . She looks tired. Her cords are dirty and she is more quiet than usual. I have a conference with her mom on Friday. I tell her it's good to have her back. She smiles and nods. (It's good to be back!)

9:10–9:40 Monday morning GYM—Good! Why do I feel as though I need a break already?

The longer Jerry wrote, the more aware he became of teaching, happenings at school, and interactions with others. He felt that this increasing attention to detail and unfolding events was largely a function of his growing habit of approaching his teaching life "as if I was going to write about it even when I'm not planning to." Though generally beneficial, this posed problems.

Over time, Jerry moved from descriptive writing to exploratory and introspective writing. His writing became less storytelling to an invisible reader and more of an inquiry for himself. His writing about the children, for example, shifted from describing and musing about them in primarily affective terms to describing in greater depth specific children and the challenges they presented to him. In the following, the first example is from early writing, the latter from later writing:

> Martha—loves me and makes no bones about it. She also "hates" school and makes no bones about that. We are working toward a medium.

> Jack—the biggest boy in my room—and the most tender in feelings boy or girl. He is beginning to mature and is more able to deal with his tender feelings. Tread LIGHTLY!

> Christina—she believes that there isn't anyone at all like me. She has her two younger sisters convinced that second grade will be all for naught if they have anyone but me for a teacher. She was redesigning her father's hair to look like mine. . . .

And later:

> Johnny Seaholt is a strange one. I wanted to shake him silly today. He gets *so* loud that I end up competing with him in the air waves. . . . He knows my expectations and often totally disregards them. I know that this affects me personally sometimes and I have to REALLY try to control myself then. I moved him off by himself today. I've eliminated those which he interacts with, but I've not solved any problem.

> Up until just two weeks ago Johnny showed no signs of caring as to whether his work was completed or not, whether the children were hurt at his expense or not, whether he missed a recess or movie to complete work or not. He has just begun to show signs of wanting to belong & be accepted. He started a shoving match on the playground last week & ended up slapping a kid on the face—and apologized for it!

> As I review my writings . . . I see more and more the need for patience. Furthermore, I am seeing patience as a practiced art. . . .

How often do I respond in the classroom when I should be biting my tongue and practicing patience? I have to wonder about my role [as teacher] as teller.

Initially, Jerry's journal, in contrast to Carole's, contained relatively little mention of his frustrations. It wasn't as if challenges didn't exist; he just didn't attempt to think them through on paper as he did in later journal entries. When he expressed frustration it was related to issues beyond his school and classroom, such as teacher education (lack of real-world experiences), the affective dimensions of teaching, and the lack of government support for schools and teachers. Although his journal did not become a dumping ground for frustration and anger, he began to write about bothersome matters that affected him directly: confrontation over lunch rules and the possible loss of a close colleague through enrollment decline in the school. After several pages where he calmly and carefully describes a difference of opinion over lunchroom policy and his perceptions of it as a waste of valuable staff meeting time and an unnecessary power struggle, Jerry writes:

Well, shit! Do you know what we didn't discuss at staff meeting? The state inspection we are having this year. . . . I am a professional. I try to get along with everyone—even the teachers I dislike—for we each hold the same goals. When I am treated like this . . . it gets under my skin. My anger has passed, yet I can't help but wonder when this little incident will be flung right back in my face, full force.

and:

Without a preface, this next writing may certainly seem subjective and judgmental. . . . I haven't a clear cut direction for this discussion, though I've thought about it for almost two weeks now. Yesterday, as I talked with Marty [a first-year teacher], I knew I must put it down, if for no other reason than to clarify the thoughts and feelings in my own being.

M: I get all new chairs for my room next year, *if* I'm here next year!

J: (apprehensively) *If* you're here? It's strange you should mention that. . . . I sure hope that you are here!

M: If the numbers are right (enough kids for a 10th section) then I'll be here, if not, I may go to third grade. (she student taught there [another building])

J: Maybe someone will retire, like Sue.

Jerry writes about Marty's professional characteristics and contrasts these with teachers whom he would "turn out to pasture":

> [I]t makes me angry. Even as I write, I find it hard to accept. . . . I think I'll take a break—re-read this and try to make some sense of it.
>
> I reread what I wrote about Marty. The facts are, I suppose, that I admire her ability, truthfulness and desire to teach. . . . I feel she is an asset professionally. . . .

The combination of writing and collegial discussion was important to Jerry. Though initial writing was "for myself only," he slowly began to share his ideas and selected writing with other teachers. He discovered the significance of professional dialogue and the importance of trust to personal and collegial reflection. Writing and discussion supported his professional development.

> I'm glad to know I do not stand alone. . . . [D]efending one's position often calls for *reflection and close inspection*. Even while wrestling with my own feelings and motives verbally, I was always received with compassion and understanding. No better feeling than to trust one's peers enough to strip the veneer which masks your motives; inspect yourself and redress, to face tomorrow a bit more prepared.

Sometimes Jerry stated problems before he wrote about them; at other times he wrote first. During a particularly difficult time, one week into the beginning of a new school year, he wrote reflectively on his military service:

> Last night I longed, even yearned for New Mexico . . . a little semi arid town nestled in the foothills of a mountain range . . . it is where I was when I found myself and gained some sense of peace within. . . . I was young, dumb and scared. . . .
>
> . . . Many days were spent hiking through the foothills and doing target practice at the local dump. I killed more tin cans in those years than one could imagine. My best memories and the catalyst for growth were the times which we would talk to the sky and greet the stars as old friends. There's nothing quite as beautiful as a southwestern sky. At night when the air is clear and the sky is cloudless one cannot help but feel small, even humble. . . . While ascending the mountain, we were transformed . . . we would pass around the mix and talk of whatever we wished,

and we covered damn near every subject imaginable. We talked
of fears, loves, hates, favorites, work, play, pleasure, the past, the
present and our future.

. . . I felt or knew no fear in telling my friends and that vast
space of sky every detail of my life, my being. And in the quiet
wee hours of the morning when we would head back to reality I
never felt less than grand. . . . It made life clear and simple. I
loved my friends and I loved myself. Last night I was desperate
for New Mexico.

A week later Jerry shared his writing with the project group. As he
talked and listened to others, he began to connect his reflective writing of
the past with his present circumstances. He found himself writing more
"philosophically." He found it much more difficult to write at all. This
was a turning point in his writing. In the following excerpt from his
discussion in the seminar, we see how he reflects on the present and on
his writing about the past. His writing becomes more introspective and
more integrative of his home and school. His longing for a place to
connect with the sky and friends parallels the uncertainty of a new school
year and a growing awareness of himself as a teacher. Responsibility
looms large, not only at school, but also at home as wife, daughter, and
young son begin the school year in different schools.

Jerry: That just hit me. They [my writings] started out . . . informal, very
descriptive, very fluid, and flowing. Then now, the beginning of this year
they are almost, um, they have come from almost a descriptive approach to a philosophical-type view of what the heck's going on. . . .
Judy: Now you're stopping to look at it.
Jerry: And myself.
Judy: Sometimes I don't like that so much; how much should we be
made to look at ourselves in depth and question who we are and what
we're about? How good is that?

Jerry: The night it hit me I wrote about New Mexico. That explains it;
see, I couldn't even explain, I see that now. [He reads the New Mexico
excerpt aloud.] I was enveloped by the sky . . . down there it made
you feel microscopic; it put you in perspective to what you actually
were, and it's where I really came to know myself and like myself . . .
talk . . . and complete trust. And it was like exorcism . . . getting
everything out of me that I didn't like. I don't know how to explain
it but . . . my writing changing from this colorful prose that I started
out with to this very philosophical, very nitpicky about me, and I stop
at the middle step in school and think, "Now what am I doing?" I

never did that before, and to what point is that good and where does it become detrimental? And I start seeing all the nitpicky things about myself that I don't like. . . . All of a sudden I'm changing myself a lot, or thinking. . . . It's this process, that's why I couldn't write this year. I refused to go any deeper into myself, I see that now . . . in writing . . . we are questioning ourselves . . . and I think there is very little precedent set for us to do that. Yet I think when we look at the whole concept of professional growth, that's a piece of it. Yes, you have to do it.

Commenting on his writing and professional growth at the end of the project, Jerry wrote:

[T]he journal was a close inspection. A chance, a delightful chance for me to speak my subjective mind and have someone actually read it. It makes all the difference in the world. It was often a chore. I realize, now, because I didn't necessarily want to confront myself. The journal offered insights and revealed a lot of my inner self to me. It admits that I care and commits me to my observations. Scary in a way. How often do we question ourselves?

. . . I've grown reflective. I move a bit slower—to savor instead of merely taste. I enjoy. I yield. I trust myself more.

SECTION III

Understanding Experience

The joy of the ride, even more than the arrival, is the motive force behind the artist's work.

E. W. Eisner

Writing well is an artistic process. While few of us consider ourselves artists with the written word, journal writing *is* directed by a sense of aesthetic balance and a continuing curiosity about life, a creative tension between an inner self and an outer world expressed in words, a personal story constructed by the author.

Now that we have described logs, diaries, and journals and their uses, and looked into the journals of three teachers, we are ready to look more closely at how words can be used to make sense of our lives as educators. Words are symbols that stand for experience, tools for classification and communication—for conveying images, capturing aspects of reality. In this section, the concept of words as vehicles for thinking and communicating is presented, and several different types of writing commonly found in educators' journals are described.

CHAPTER 6

Exploring
with Words

Human experience is brought into being through language.

Paulo Freire

COMMUNICATION, COGNITION, AND SYMBOL SYSTEMS

Trying to make sense of life is often referred to as cognition, "the act or process of knowing" (*Merriam-Webster Dictionary*). It is a complex process. According to Freud (1961), we know on multiple levels: the unconscious, subconscious, and conscious. To complicate matters, we are unaware of most of what we know. Polanyi (1967), for example, describes knowledge that we have but cannot articulate as tacit knowledge. We know far more than we can put into words; we sense and understand more than we can describe. This can be seen in infancy: an infant is receptive to others' verbalizations long before he or she can speak.

Knowing more than we know we know serves important functions in making sense of life and in adapting to it. Much of our behavior is routine and taken for granted; we don't think about it consciously, we simply act. Tripp (1984) calls this functioning on "autopilot." It enables us to live without having to attend to recurring details. We learn from experience and act automatically. This works until there is discord or a mismatch between the circumstances and our automatic responses. In driving, for example, we are not usually conscious of our actions until some split-second emergency arises. Automatic actions are useful because they free our minds from having to think about routine activities, allowing us to learn, and yet they can be overridden when the need arises. However, routines can become too comfortable. While we seek knowledge and change, we also protect ourselves against them. As Scott-Maxwell (1968) writes, "We are blind, we prefer to be blind. It is easier" (p. 85). We retreat to safety when we feel threatened, overwhelmed, or out of step with those around us.

Change is often threatening. According to Kelley (1947), what is perceived depends on three attributes: biology (what we are able to perceive physically and psychologically), past experiences (what we are prepared to perceive), and motivations (what moves us to want to perceive). We act from situational perceptions. When we are comfortable with ourselves and our present circumstances, we are free to explore the world around us. In contrast, when we feel threatened, we use our energies to defend ourselves from perceived dangers; we are not free to explore.

Kelly (1955) describes cognitive structures, or "constructs," as relatively permeable or impermeable. When we feel at ease, we have permeable constructs; when we feel threatened, our constructs become less permeable. Our focus narrows; we are too busy protecting ourselves to be "confused by the facts." When our constructs are permeable, or flexible, we can use our energy to explore; we can march into new territory and thrive on novelty, open ourselves to challenge and re-explore familiar territory from fresh perspectives. This process can be seen when we observe toddlers in a preschool setting: some beam at their mothers as they head for colorful toys, while others, unsure of themselves and their new environment, cling. Slowly, these more reluctant children begin to explore visually and then physically the new environment—with mother in close proximity. The more secure they feel, the more free they are to venture forth.

Learning takes place as a result of experience. As we engage in meaningful experience, changes in perception enable further learning to take place. Change in schemata, in the way we look at something, occurs. New horizons for inquiry open to us; our content is the world. The languages of various forms of representation open different aspects and ways to interpret the world. Each language presents its own nonredundant perspective: the arts, physical sciences, social sciences, and humanities. Each form of representation (literature, dance, mathematics, astronomy, painting) offers unique ways to interpret phenomena; each offers a way of organizing and interrelating different aspects of life. Each offers a different language for communication—a bridge by which to explore experience with others.

Like artists and scientists, we try to reduce the bombardment of stimuli and form connections that make sense. We simplify our lives by using symbols, models, and frames of reference to communicate with others and to integrate our knowledge. We interpret life through those forms of representation that we understand. Though painting, dance, literature, and mathematics are never the same as our experiences, they enable us to bring multiple dimensions of life to a conscious level where we can ponder them. For example, numbers help us determine how much carpet is needed to cover a floor; aesthetic sensibility informs our choice of color, texture, and style. Through these languages we discuss ideas and feelings; we hypothesize and reflect.

Language separates us from all other creatures. It offers unique opportunities for reflecting on life. We are alone with the knowledge of our history, our awareness of a past and a future, and our capacity to understand many of the natural forces that shape and delimit life on earth. We are alone because we can imagine with and in words. Walker Percy writes on language and knowing in a book entitled *The Message in the Bottle: How Queer Man Is, How Queer Language Is, and What One Has to Do with the Other* (1954). He poses many questions about humankind and language, among them:

> Why is it that men speak and animals don't?
> What does it entail to be a speaking creature . . . ?
> Why is there such a gap between nonspeaking animals and speaking man, when there is no other such gap in nature?
> How can a child learn to speak a language in three years without anyone taking trouble about it, that is, utter and understand an unlimited number of sentences, while a great deal of time and trouble is required to teach a chimpanzee a few hand signals?
> Is it possible that a theory of man is nothing more nor less than a theory of the speaking creature? (8)

Naturalist Loren Eiseley (1978) ponders similar thoughts:

> All animals which man has reason to believe are more than usually intelligent—our relatives the great apes, the elephant, the raccoon, the wolverine, among others—are problem solvers, and in at least a small way manipulators of their environment. Save for the instinctive calls of their species, however, they cannot communicate except by direct imitation. They cannot invent words for new situations nor get their fellows to use such words. No matter how high the individual intelligence, its private world remains a private possession locked forever within a single, perishable brain. (42)

We use words to make sense of our culture's forms of representation. Language, in fact, is at the base of several of them, and without it, many forms of representation would not be available, for words provide a major way of drawing together and integrating experiences on both conscious and unconscious levels. Writing enables connections to the past—the continuing story of humankind.

> Man without writing cannot long retain his story in his head. His intelligence permits him to grasp some kind of succession of generations; but without writing, the tale of the past rapidly degenerates into fumbling myth and fable. Man's greatest epic, his four long battles with the advancing ice of the great continental glaciers, has vanished from human memory without a trace. . . .
>
> Writing, and later printing, is the product of our adaptable many-purposed hands. It is thus, through writing . . . that modern man carries in his mind the intellectual triumphs of all his predecessors who were able to inscribe their thoughts for posterity. (Eiseley 1978, 41–42)

JOURNAL WRITING, THE MIND, AND SELF-KNOWLEDGE

Since writing taps tacit knowledge, it is more powerful than it might seem to be. Writing about an issue that concerns us necessitates our forming thoughts that had, until then, been implicit. In the act of writing we express what we sense or intuit, and often what we didn't know we knew. We clarify for ourselves what had been confusing and we "come to [new] conclusions and ideas about courses of action to take. . . . We should not be surprised that unconscious material surfaces so readily . . . writing stimulates this interchange and allows us to observe, direct, and understand it" (Ferrucci 1982, 41). And, although directing or redirecting aspects of our lives and teaching is, in Ferrucci's words, "like cutting a new pathway in the jungle" (42), it is possible. For, having fully recognized patterns in ourselves and how we adapt to and shape our circumstances in ways that no longer appear to be useful (and are at odds with our aims), change is already in motion; "Any pattern that is discovered—and fully surfaced, changes . . . it is then possible to replace destructive tendencies with more functional ones" (Ferrucci 1982, 42).

Writing is empowering because it "allows us to observe, direct, and understand" what we write about. Writing focuses our attention, holds it, and, if we return to the writing later, makes learning more likely. This is related to how the mind functions. Writing facilitates consciousness of consciousness (what Dewey termed "awareness"); it introduces the author to the many minds that inform practice. As Ornstein (1988) wrote:

> Instead of a single, intellectual entity that can judge many different kinds of events equally, the mind is diverse and complex. It contains a changeable conglomeration of different kinds of "small minds"—fixed reactions, talents, flexible thinking and these entities are temporarily employed—"wheeled into consciousness"—and then usually discarded, returned to their place after use. (25)

Which of these "small minds" gets wheeled in depends on our circumstances. According to Ornstein:

> We are built to respond simply and quickly. Our judgment process operates by a set of fast paths; we build external categories to simplify our perceptions and judgments based on a network of invisible structures. We are primed to respond to what's on at the moment and sometimes we over-react. We are primed by emotion and alertness or action to avoid emergencies. . . . Anything that is given wide publicity in the media . . . get[s] fast reactions while constant problems get ignored. . . . [W]e remain unaware because we do not understand the complexity within ourselves. . . . Tragedies exist within ourselves due to a lack of communication within the separated components of the mind. (32)

The journal enables us to observe our reactions (and minds), and the more aware of these we become, the more aware of our present circumstances we become. Having touched a burner on the stove, for example, the more aware we are the next time we come near it, and therefore the more careful we are and the more control over our movements we have. Just as we type, or simplify, our views of ourselves in characteristics, we do the same to others ("the quiet child," "the slow learner"). This simplifies teaching and at the same time makes it more difficult, because "each one of us is a crowd of people" (Ornstein 1988, 185). Once a characteristic or type or category has been adopted, it is very difficult to see beyond it; it directs our perceiving and becomes a comfortable or secure framework that allows us to attend to other matters (of which there are always a surfeit), even if these images are ones we would prefer not to hold.

The different "small minds" often have their own priorities, which can be at odds with one another and with the demands of our highly developed civilization. While a teacher would like to pay more attention to "the quiet child," this becomes lost in a myriad of other demands. Whether or not attending to this child in a focused way is more important than collecting milk money or having a conference with a parent or cleaning the goldfish bowl is not usually a question. With careful deliberation or focused thought on one's priorities, the teacher in question may choose to use her energies in different ways. "It would be a good idea, I think," writes Ornstein, "if we could come to see the primitive bases of many of our judgments and decisions so that we might try to do something about them" (24). We can observe our own behavior and direct it consciously rather than continuing on "autopilot." Given the increasingly full and standardized nature of curriculum development and teaching today, and the press to accomplish more and sooner (Elkind 1983), it is even more necessary to take time out to observe what we are doing, to see which minds are wheeled in so that we can begin to take a more professional and directive role in our own activity. As Ornstein (1988) writes:

> It is a question of who is running the show. In most people, at most times, the automatic system . . . organizes which small mind gets wheeled in, most likely the automatic bases of blind habit. But there is a point when a person can become conscious of the multiminds and begin to run them. (185)

As journal writing becomes a habit, it can also become a process for remaining a "stranger," one who is open to what happens and to the mysteries that unfold in even the most common of everyday occurrences. As Ruth put it, "This writing and reviewing our writing is surprisingly educational. I thought I was knowledgeable about myself. I keep finding facets I didn't realize existed" (journal excerpt, 1981).

CHAPTER 7

Types of Journal Writing

I am happy to be both halves, the watcher and the watched.

Albert Camus

JOURNALISTIC WRITING

Journalistic writing is essentially descriptive. A journalist describes events and circumstances as an outside observer. Only events and circumstances perceived to be relevant to the topic are included—and then as parsimoniously as possible. Questions such as who, what, when, where, how, and why guide the journalist's inquiry. When facts are interpreted, it is usually made obvious to the reader that these are interpretations. It is the journalist's job to document and describe carefully so that the reader may draw her or his own conclusion.

Todd Benham, a middle school vocational education teacher, for example, takes the first month of school to write brief, descriptive portraits of new students. Each day he writes a few sentences about several students. As the year progresses he adds information. He finds this documentation helpful in evaluating student progress and in providing him with ideas on how to build on students' experiences. A rather fuzzy portrait becomes a more distinctive picture as new information adds definition. Todd initially found it difficult to be descriptive without being judgmental. He doesn't worry much about this anymore; in rereading the portraits he can see where his opinions enter into the writing.

The following example is excerpted from a case study in a first-year teacher's journal. Here Trudy Prescott collects descriptive information for later analysis. She notes in log fashion what she perceives to be important information related to the subject of her study, a fifth-grade child named Jason. She begins with contextual information and then logs the child's behavior. At the end of each day's log she summarizes and offers her general interpretation of the flow of the day.

2/6

Jason is one of the two white children in our class . . . is slightly overweight and is of average height . . . a little more intellectual than most in our class. He enjoys things that lead to enquiry and creativity. Jason does not like to do things that are not to his liking . . . verbal complaints are common when this occurs. . . . I have tried seating him in various ways and in a matter of time he is begging to be moved. Verbal arguments are very frequent. Outbursts about how he hates our class [are] common. Twice he has cried over his lack of friends. . . .

2/10

9:25 Entered very quietly—sprained wrist.
9:45 Raised hand to ask questions. Working intently on spelling.
10:30 Sitting by himself—working quietly on computer, helping another student.
1:45 Making silly noises. Seemed to like the attention. Reprimanded.
3:00 Worked on task for the rest of the day.

Jason did not make any complaints about school today. He was on task and pleasant. At 1:45, when he started to be disruptive, a casual reminder of how hard he had been working put him back on target.

2/11

. . .
10:30 Created a detailed pattern for his haiku.
12:00 On task—No arguing.
1:30 Came back from lunch upset—wouldn't say why.
2:30 Helping him clean out his desk. I saw a note that was complaining about school and me. Got immediately upset when he realized I saw it.
2:30–3:30 Repeatedly verbalizing how he didn't care about a contest we were having. Would not do his health. Found unfinished reading papers in his desk. When I asked where his reading folder was he said he tore it up because he hates reading.
3:30–3:45 Crying when he left. Verbal argument w/Bryson. Said he couldn't stay to talk.

Jason was a little crabby this morning but he seemed to be in control of it. He did not take his mood out on others. Instead, he got straight to work.

I assume something must have happened on the playground. Although, reflecting back, he seemed to get himself under control again.

The factor that seemed to initiate his poor behavior was when I saw the note he had written. I think he cares about me even though he professes not to. If he didn't care he wouldn't be upset I saw the note.

As Trudy logs Jason's behavior, she acts as a journalist: what does he do? what are the facts surrounding his action? As she continues to log information, she becomes more detailed in her descriptions. For example, she began to note specifically what he did when he was "on task." She paid more attention to how he entered the room each morning and what he said. And she more closely noted her own behavior and thinking: "When I thought he was having trouble controlling himself after lunchtime I asked him if he could help me set up the science center. He looked surprised, smiled faintly, and started softly hitting one hand into the other in a tap, taaap rhythm. Looking around (to see who was looking?) he followed me to the table." As she kept the journal, she reviewed the information and began to share what she was doing with a colleague, who was able to pose questions that she might not have come to on her own: "What do you mean when you write that he is 'more intellectual than most. . . . I wonder if the lunch monitor could provide some additional information about his interactions at lunchtime'?"

In the daily summaries and interpretive comments, the teacher begins to reflect on and analyze both the child's actions and her own, which brings us to analytical writing.

ANALYTICAL WRITING

When writing analytically, the writer focuses on specific aspects or dimensions of the topic under study. Attention is directed to their nature and possible relationships. For example, does Jason's behavior during lunchtime seem to be related to his behavior in school that afternoon, or when is he on task and when is he off task? What other factors might be related? When the teacher is successful in redirecting his attention to schoolwork, how has it come about? How might the ways she tries to redirect his attention vary from one circumstance to another? This type of writing is a form of reasoning and clarifying the subject under study. Through analysis, important aspects of the topic can become apparent. The teacher finds that she is more often successful in influencing Jason's behavior when she asks him if he will help her by finishing his work rather than when she tells him more directly to finish it.

Analytical writing usually begins with a problem that defies immediate solution. In the following journal excerpt, we see Craig defining and analyzing a problem that began as a vague sense that something wasn't quite right.

> I was ambushed in late afternoon in a conference that I viewed as a formality and courtesy. I talk to the mother three or four times a week on an informal basis since she is very active in school programs. Near the end of our time she asks "Do you think there is something strange about Melody?" What a shot! There has been a feeling I could never grasp but always disturbing that, yes, something is strange about Melody and not in a positive sense. She does not seem to be a whole child but I could never lead myself past vague generalities to broach the subject with anyone, especially her mom. Now, Mom's scored a direct hit and knows it from my undisciplined reaction and I am thoroughly befuddled. I don't want to talk about it, even though it's a real problem, because I have nothing to say that I can back up concretely. I decide to try and listen to see what I can find out but no way, Mom wants to hear from me and not talk herself. We get nowhere and we stop with me having the awareness that she feels she has done something terrible to her daughter. I feel terrible about it and worry into the night about how to mend some hurt. The next day Melody volunteers that I hurt her Mom's feelings. Just great! I sent a note home with Melody telling her that, in my opinion, she was an excellent mother (True!) and that we should make plans for further discussion.
>
> Now I'm committed to figuring this puzzle out before we talk again.
>
> Melody is spotless jumpers, fancy blouses, patent leather shoes, socks with no holes, and freshly curled blond hair. . . . Melody shares, cares for her friends, isn't bossy and never gets in trouble or causes anyone else to have difficulty. The children regret that she has only two sides since that limits the number of people who can sit by her. . . .
>
> Melody and her younger brother and sister, but especially Melody, are the apples of their Mom's eye. I don't know the father at all. She takes them everywhere, they are obedient and polite and the objects of many flattering comments which Mom accepts graciously. Even the two-year-old is always spotlessly clean, neat and well behaved. . . .

What is disturbing about Melody?

1. An almost complete lack of creativity.
2. Interest and curiosity well below what you would expect in view of her skills.
3. Success in closed-ended endeavors with a definable, obvious goal (Letterbooks, canned art projects, recall tasks) but withdrawal from open-ended discussions, problem solving activities and flights of fancy that are just for fun.
4. No affective skills other than the power of her lovely presence.
5. No emotional displays—even accidentally peeing on herself did not erase the half-smile from her face. I did, however, see her cry one day when she got confused about where she was supposed to meet her mother after school but that's all.

I think I know what it is. Melody has been systematically robbed of many childhood pleasures. I spend so much time working with kids who are 5 and act 3 that I failed to realize that here was a five-year-old who acted nine. I forgot the coin has two sides. Melody had been expected to act and look like a little lady. Two younger siblings reinforce her view of herself as grown-up. Mom has dedicated her last 5–6 years *completely* to her children and she wants them to be perfect. Melody has had all the tribulations of childhood but none of the trials. She has had the very best of toys but (I'm conjecturing) always told precisely how to use them. . . . She's never played outside in the rain, stomped in every mud puddle, climbed a tree or had the satisfaction of kicking her little brother in the teeth. Mom wanted Miss Perfect and by all outward appearances she got it. If it *appears* perfect it must be.

The preceding paragraph is a hypothesis that will be difficult to prove. Advancing it to Mom puts me on very thin ice and is harshly judgmental of her child rearing practices. . . .

The very fact that she brought up Melody's "strangeness" indicates she is aware of some difficulty and is calling for help. Happily, a five-year-old cannot be completely robbed of childhood with so many years of it still ahead. I'm going to suggest that she begin sending her to school in jeans and T-shirts, forget the hairdos and send her out to play in the mud this Spring. Seek her opinion[s], explore them with her and. . . . Don't provide all the structure for her, leave her to create her own and learn to accommodate it.

As Craig describes the problem he clarifies different aspects of it. When Melody's mother poses the question, he realizes what he has not yet been able to put into words. He gathers facts about the child and the circumstances by putting them on paper. As he sees the puzzle take shape he begins hypothesizing, stepping beyond facts—"conjecturing." Although he doesn't take his thinking to the point of introspection—what he might do to contribute to the problem, or how he might test his hypotheses and help to better define and resolve the problem—now he has some facts, some hypotheses, some possible actions. By writing the facts as he sees them, he becomes aware of problems that other children in his room might have—being hurried, pushed, and therefore deprived of childhood. The "good" child (the one who poses no outward problems) becomes the one to observe. Craig had been unable to talk to anyone about the problem because he couldn't yet put it into words, nor did he want to appear ignorant ("Mom's scored a direct hit and knows it from my undisciplined reaction"). But in his journal he has the luxury of describing and analyzing until he has the words and the inclination to talk with someone.

EVALUATIVE WRITING

Evaluation is a means of assigning value to phenomena. Writing as a form of evaluation includes analyzing and synthesizing information. Whereas analyzing necessitates taking apart elements for examination, synthesizing involves integrating them. Both processes are important to evaluation. There are two basic types of evaluation: *formative*, which informs us of progress along the way; and *summative*, which is conducted at the conclusion of an activity. With formative evaluation we can change our plan if need be; we can take advantage of information gained during the evaluation process. It is a way of monitoring. Formative writing involves documentation of problem solving. Summative writing helps to define what, if anything, happened as a result of effort: both planned and unanticipated changes. Evaluative writing can aid the author in determining a person's or program's progress toward a valued end, while it can also be used to refine (and redefine) the end. As Macrorie (1984) put it: "Writing is a way of thinking, of objectifying an act that has meaning. . . . As the sentences go down on the page, they become both finished statements and starting points for reflection and evaluation. The passages grow with thought" (preface).

Jeanette McConnell is a high school art teacher who frequently uses her journal for evaluation. Recently, for example, she has been concerned with a decrease in the number of students electing to take art classes. She has several ideas about why and decides to look for answers. She will interview other teachers, students, and artists and look more closely at the art curriculum and its relevance to students. Does the curriculum need to be reconceptualized? Are there cultural factors beyond the school that might be related? What steps, if any, can she take to alleviate any problems she defines? Where should she direct her energies? Jeanette begins her search by writing about the problem and how she might approach it. "Over the last three years the enrollment in art has dropped almost 28 percent while the student population has increased by 9 percent. . . . I can find out how students view art, ask them how they decide to sign up for specific courses." With this information she can reformulate her inquiry and map out ways to study the problem(s). As she takes action she documents what happens and uses this as formative evaluation. During the interviews many students said without hesitation, "Art isn't a requirement for college admittance. I have to take courses that are." Now Jeanette better understands the problem and can explore these findings with other art teachers.

Evaluative writing can be as simple and straightforward as documenting lesson plans, then evaluating what happened; or it can be as complex as evaluating the documentation of planning and implementation of a curricular program. In the following example Tom reflects on the day in an evaluative way and ends by giving himself advice.

10/20 Mon (eve.)
Don't come into the school with too many things on your agenda. Today I did just such a foolish thing. I unloaded the car (four trips) which included the usual gear, plans, books and paper, plus a bale of hay, and a bundle of corn stalks (7 feet tall). The plans. Oh the plans I had for this day. I was going to have a mother-aide do this, the mother-aide do that. Five minutes before the kids arrive I get a note from the office telling me I would be without an aide for the morning.

This made a normally super busy day even more so. My unit on leaves is limping along. I'm playing catch-up to get enough information to chart for the first grading period reports. I don't have any breaks on Mondays. I crammed a lot of work in and brought most of it home. More is less. I keep saying it but also keep stuffing the curriculum. Next nine weeks is going to be less busy. I'll slow down, the kids will benefit.

Tom's evaluation is formative (these things interact to cause problems; I can still work on the unit and collect information for the grade report), as well as being a summative evaluation of the day.

ETHNOGRAPHIC WRITING

This type of writing is grounded in the writer's observations, experience, and study of a person, or people, in a specific social and cultural environment. It originated in anthropology as researchers sought to describe people, customs, and artifacts within their social and cultural contexts. Ethnographic writing is phenomenological (seeking to describe phenomena from the meanings that people ascribe to their experience), comparative (both within a culture and cross-culturally), analytical (carefully studying persons and culture as they may relate to one another), and creative (drawing together, integrating seemingly diverse dimensions of experience to convey a picture of the whole). The researcher seeks to capture the dynamics, the sense of the subject under study within the native environment.

Educators and educational researchers have used ethnographic techniques in studying students, teachers, and schools for years. In fact, the case study method and naturalistic study in general have experienced a resurgence over the past several years. *The Good High School* (Lightfoot 1983), *A Place Called School* (Goodlad 1984), and Robert Coles' (1967, 1971a, 1971b, 1977a, 1977b) Pulitzer Prize-winning series, *Children of Crisis*, are all based on ethnographic research.

As an inquirer into his own practice, Craig studies both his teaching and the larger contexts within which he works. In an attempt to describe his school to people who have never seen it, he tries to stand outside and look keenly at it, and he also tries to include the feelings he has from working inside:

> It could be right out of a real estate ad. Traditional, 20 rooms, four baths, large lot, atop a hill in rural Northridge County. Actually, it is my school, a rather conspicuous red brick structure that makes me feel young. Hoover has most of the things that all schools have—a flag pole, lots of sidewalks that are worn away around the edges and will probably be widened one day (soon there will be no grass) and of course, areas to accommodate those hulking yellow monsters that disgorge children each morning only to ingest them again a few hours later. You may be late for school, forget to do your lesson plans, or refuse to teach reading, but don't park in the bus turnaround.
>
> The interior of the building is rather like the lining of my oldest winter coat, an indeterminate color and fading fast. It's dark and very uninteresting—lockers and more lockers and rarely anything to see or do in the halls. I'm glad I don't teach in a school where exterior bulletin board competitions occupied my time, but Hoover hallways could be spruced up a bit. . . .

Most parents genuinely want a good education for their children but do not know how to contribute toward that end. Their own negative school experiences are a block and it takes a lot of patience and understanding to involve them in their children's programs. They are basically good people caught in the pressure cooker of semi-poverty. Day-to-day existence is a preoccupation undermining any long-term goals or visions. . . .

We are 15 self-contained classrooms . . . for a staff of 22. There is a deep and disturbing division in our staff. We cannot function as a group so we rarely have staff meetings, and then, only to discuss procedural matters. We are so at odds with one another that neither group could really accept an idea from the other, no matter how good.

One group has been at Hoover forever. Sometimes I think the classrooms were built around them. Then, there are those of us, who, after five years are still considered new teachers—outsiders. . . .

Ethnographic writing can be difficult; it's hard to sift out opinions and inferences from interpretations. Once we have a stake in what we are describing, it's hard to be objective. This is why we build in safeguards and techniques like triangulation (comparing multiple sources of data), where we look to multiple data sources for corroboration and discrepancies. Craig, for example, wrote the description of Hoover school from his point of view. Were he to ask other teachers, perhaps an administrator, or parents to read and comment on it, he would be testing his perceptions and observations against theirs. If they read it and said, "Yes, that is my school!" he would have gained consensus. If he found differences of opinion he might have to rethink his descriptions, perhaps rewrite and consult with other people for their opinions.

Ethnographic journal writing includes recording facts and descriptions of classroom activities, interactions of students, and our own behavior. At the simplest level it involves recording and describing. It can also evolve into articulating vivid pictures of classroom life, learning and teaching, and people. Ethnography is a "swing" type of writing between the previous types already mentioned and those that follow. It is an integration of descriptive, outside-the-self focusing and reflective, introspective, self-aware writing. A colleague, for example, might ask Craig how he knows that "parents genuinely want a good education for their children." Then, he has the opportunity to step back and probe more deeply; he revisits his original observations.

Teachers are, by the nature of teaching, inquirers. When the curiosity that sparks inquiry is carried forward in a deliberate and self-aware fashion, it becomes research. Perhaps one of the more articulate teacher-researchers who wrote about teaching in her diaries (we would call them journals here) is Sylvia Ashton-Warner. Writing as an ethnographer with an artist's keenly observant eye, she illuminates "ordinary" classroom life from the participant's perspective:

"Jacob, bring me your exercise book. Let me see it."

"Please I . . . please it's not here."

"Where is it?"

"Please at home."

"I told you not to take your book home. You'll have to go home and get it. Up you get . . . off! Go home and get your book."

"Please I can't."

"You've got legs!"

"Please yes. But the canoe it's not there."

"What's the canoe got to do with it?"

"My grandfather took it."

"Where?"

"Please he took our canoe downriver to the other pa [Maori village] because there's a tangi [Maori funeral] there because a man got drowned last night. He was eeling."

"What have eels got to do with your exercise book?"

Tiny beside me, who is truly tiny like a little black beetle, said, "Please Jacob he live on the other side of the river. He comes to schools in the canoe."

"Am I to believe that a boy of Jacob's size goes to and fro across that wide deep river in a canoe every day?"

"Please, my big sisters bring me. They in Mr. Hen'son's room."

I paused. I'd lost the thread. With elbow on table I covered my eyes with a hand while I tried to find it again but all I could see in my mind were canoes, drowned men, eels and a grandfather. "What was I talking about, Tiny?"

She brushed the black hair from her eyes. "Please about Jacob he hasn't did his writing."

Mercifully the bell rang for morning play. . . .

"Really," to K [husband, the principal] over morning tea, "my teaching. I haven't started to teach. There's no communication. We're supposed to be using the same language but we just don't understand each other. I dunno. . . ."

". . . [Y]ou see they're not thinking about what they're writing about or about what I'm teaching. I'm teaching about 'bed' and 'can' but they were thinking about canoes and grandfathers and drowned men and eels. It seems to me . . . I seem rude to intrude."

"That's just it. Well, dear, that's what we're paid to do, just that: intrude."

Intrude. For once I won't intrude. It's really time for reading about the bed, the can, and I can jump, I can skip and I can run. But I can't bring myself to do it. I'll follow them into their own minds and fraternize there; their minds are full of grandfathers, canoes and eels and the river and so, indeed, is mine. (1966, 21–23)

Observing and writing about the children and life in the classroom enables the author to put some of the challenges of teaching into perspective. In the next excerpt we see how Ashton-Warner hypothesizes about the problem of curriculum relevance and how she tries to solve the problem by creating a set of reading books that address the challenges she writes about above.

The distance between the content of their minds, however, and the content of our reading books is nothing less than frightening. I can't believe that Janet and John never fall down and scratch a knee and run crying to Mummy. I don't know why their mother never kisses them or calls them "darling." Doesn't John ever disobey? Has the American child no fears? Does it never rain or blow in America? Why is it always fine in primer books? If these questions are naive it must be because of the five-year-old company I keep. Heaven knows we have enough lively incident in our Maori infant rooms. The fights, the loveships, and the uppercuts from the newcomers. I see the respectable happy reading book placed like a lid upon this—ignoring, hiding and suppressing it.

Into the text and pictures of these transitional books I have let a little of the drama through. A few of the tears. A good bit of the fears, some of the love, and an implication for the culture. From the rich soil of the Key Vocabulary [from the children's words] and the creative writing I can do no less. Even if I did deplore dramatic living, which I don't. To me it is life complete with its third dimension and since Beethoven and Tchaikovsky see it the same way, I am this time in more august company. (1966, 67–69)

THERAPEUTIC WRITING

Whether or not it is intended to be, most journal writing is therapeutic (Stillman 1987). Writing for therapeutic purposes, as Mallon's (1984) pilgrims discover, can be an important aid to personal and professional growth. It taps our inner selves and provides a way to work through professional problems and personal challenges. It can be quick, free-flowing, spontaneous, or slow, meditative, and analytical. It can, in other words, be expanded and edited during times of calm.

Writing about our lives and documenting how we adapt to the pressures we encounter as educators enables us to identify patterns in our behavior. It is almost like reading about someone else. As we re-examine our journals, we can become increasingly more self-accepting and less judgmental. Once we see the broader context within which we acted, our behavior makes sense. What might now be viewed as a mistake seemed logical at the time. With self-acceptance comes self-trust. To take this one step further, there is evidence to suggest that as we grow in trust of ourselves we also grow in trust of others. In a study of a small group of special education teachers, for example, the researchers found that as teachers became more confident and flexible in interactions with each other during university seminar sessions, they also became more confident and flexible in their teaching (Knoblock and Goldstein 1971).

In addition to using writing as an aid to gaining self-knowledge, writing can be therapeutic in at least two other ways. The process can be cathartic. Through it we can purge ourselves of pent-up emotions: "Now that I say it I don't feel it. . . . Melancholy diminishes as I write" (Woolf October 25, 1920). (There is, however, the chance that in letting our emotions out onto paper we will feel enough relief to stop short of effecting actual change.) Writing for catharsis can alleviate symptoms of problems and even promote permanent relief. Kate, for example, points out the importance of having a safe place to let off pressure: "It's difficult to relate all the feelings, intentions one has—only one's words are heard. . . . I often overstate kids' foibles just to let off pressure. . . ." In the privacy of her journal she doesn't have to worry about others misinterpreting or misusing her words.

Humor and play are among the most important resources for personal and professional development. In fact, they are probably two of the most underused and potent tools for renewal. Problems can be balanced with humor; "seriosity" dealt a felicitous blow. Humor can be used, as Craig does in this example, as relief from some of the stressful conditions in school:

Here's a test.
Moving a class from one place to another is most like:

1) The Pied Piper
2) "Rawhide" from our TV youth
3) Pickett's Charge

4) Locomotion before the invention of the wheel
5) Lemmings going over the edge
6) A civil disturbance
7) The line at the bank
8) Putting an elephant through the eye of a needle
9) The exercise period at San Quentin

When their classes are in the hall teachers are most like:

1) George Patton
2) An air traffic controller at O'Hare
3) Don Rickles
4) Helen Keller
5) A frightened ostrich
6) Jekyll
7) Hyde
8) Sherlock Holmes
9) —Hm—I wish I could think of a classic buffoon. . . .

These items need [to be] validated for use in my index of teacher behavior.

Craig began the following journal entry sardonically, but as he wrote, his mood changed, softening with recollection:

The custodian—mover of large objects, controller of the physical environment, omnipresent in the halls, keeper of the mysterious boilers, and the saint of saints when a kid pukes on your rug. He also is the zipper and stapler doctor, mechanic when your car won't start, and keeper of the clocks that all tell the same time even if it's wrong. Isn't it curious that this indispensable person whose benevolence is so carefully cultivated is the same asshole who freezes you out of your room because he thinks he pays the gas bill out of his own pocket, mows the grass outside your window while you're trying to read a story, fixes your lights during math when the kids will be going home in 10 minutes, mops the floor in the hall just when it's time to get drinks, and presides over his realm with all the jealousy and capriciousness of an aging king.

A few years ago a first grader pointed to our night custodian, who bears only marginal resemblance to a human being, and confidently asserted "See him right there. That's the boss of the whole school." . . . We can get by with teacher absence, no principal or reading specialist but without the janitor we would have to close the school. It would simply collapse under its own weight.

It's probably worth noting that I can tell you a hell of a lot more about Mr. Bennett my grade school custodian, than I could about many of my teachers. He was important. I was genuinely saddened to learn a few years ago that he had died. Lots of things change in a school but the custodian is a constant, a stabilizer in turmoil. It's impossible to think of him in a place other than the school, especially dead.

REFLECTIVE WRITING

If most journal writing is therapeutic in effect, it can also be said that much of it is reflective in nature. The author looks back in writing, sometimes as an outside observer and sometimes as an interested participant who edits and interprets experience through writing. When the Teacher Reflections project began, I asked the seven participants to reflect every day or so on their teaching and to write whatever they remembered and felt like recording. I hoped that it would be like a mirror of events in their teaching lives, everyday incidents worth looking at again and sometimes pondering. While this seemed like a rather simple task, it turned out otherwise. Bringing back images—mirroring experiences—wasn't easy. For one thing, the mirror always focused on particular aspects of experience rather than others. On one hand this is what I wanted, to find out how teachers viewed their work, not how an "objective" outsider, or camera, or mirror, would reproduce it. On the other hand, writing itself was an intervention to their thinking about practice. It was difficult to write about "anything," especially if you hadn't written about teaching before. Some of the writing was mirrorlike, but most of it at the beginning was subjectively descriptive. They wrote about children and routine classroom and curricular activities and their attendant problems and frustrations. As teachers continued to write, however, their work became more vividly descriptive, analytical, reflective, and introspective, and for some teachers, it thus became a useful tool for planning.

Pondering is a useful part of reflective writing. Reconsidering experiences brings to light new thoughts and different dimensions. Just-lived events slowly (sometimes suddenly) make sense and connect with other events, weaving into an evolving tapestry. Written reflections provide stationary yet flexible pictures that can be manipulated so that different dimensions and perspectives on experience may be exposed. As humans and perhaps especially as educators, we reflect continuously. Most of our reflections, however, are fleeting. Reflective writing enables us to ponder thoughts long enough to form connections and learn from experience.

Planning is an assumed part of teaching and administering, while conscious reflection is relatively rare. Could this be related to Virginia Woolf's (1978) point: "Why then don't I write it down oftener? Well, one's vanity forbids. I want to appear a success even to myself...." (36)? Most of us prepare written plans for our work, but how many of us reflect systematically on it? What actually happened, and how do we evaluate it? It's often that we don't think consciously about it—that we are, most of us, attuned to forward, linear movement along a course of "progress." Obviously, the other half of planning, reflecting on our experiences, deserves conscious attention too.

In its simplest form, reflective writing is like keeping a log, putting on paper what happened. In the following example Tom reflects on a week that went well. The entry is also evaluative (the week went well) and analytical (what contributed to the week's going well).

> 10/13   4:30 PM   (Mon.)
> One of the reasons last week seemed to go well was that I had lots of help. Another reason was that I didn't attempt quite as much in each day. I didn't lower my standards, just my expectations.
>
> Some of the help I received was from room mothers, and my sister and niece. Other help came from four girls who stopped in at lunch to help file papers and do color work. These kids are from the fourth and fifth grades, and they help a lot. It's amazing how much cutting four kids can get done in a half hour.

INTROSPECTIVE WRITING

Whereas reflective writing necessitates recording experiences as we look back at them, introspective writing involves the examination of our thoughts, sensory experiences, and feelings. There are many reasons for our behavior, but we rarely step back to ask ourselves, "Why did I do/feel/think that?" Present circumstances, habit, external influences, our biases and unrecognized needs and motivations can move us to behave in ways that are sometimes at variance with more deliberative aims. We are vulnerable when we question ourselves. We sometimes feel threatened by change and the discomfort that accompanies the dissonance arising from the difference between our images of ourselves and our behavior. To write introspectively means to march, if haltingly, through barriers to self-discovery, into our pasts, and to the motives and circumstances that influence our behavior. To write introspectively sometimes means to write thoughtfully and deliberately, at other times spontaneously. It incorporates many other types of writing in the observation and analysis of our mental and emotional states. In the following example, Craig writes reflectively and introspectively:

> I ask kids "why" questions but I am reluctant to answer them about myself. So I began writing around the edges, hoping the middle would drop out without a lot of effort. No way! So there is a period in the diary where I have a lot of stupid stuff, pseudo-self-analysis—form but no substance.
>
> Through some of the writing and in quiet undocumented thinking sessions I began to look at things very differently. I had spent a good deal of time reflecting on the institutional and societal functions of schooling and the art of teaching, but always it seemed as an observer. Now I was looking at myself as a participant. Seeing myself in the roles I had described in a detached manner.
>
> Things went straight to hell. No matter what, I could not resolve the question of what I was doing in a kindergarten classroom. . . .

In the next excerpt, Jerry connects events from home and school as he considers patience.

> I am seeing patience as more than a virtue, patience is a practiced art.
>
> Last evening I took my daughter, April, to the "home game" at our local high school. Actually, I dropped her off, I didn't take her. . . . April is 14 and this is a big social event for her. . . . Her plans were to meet her friend, Sandy, . . . and Sandy was to [later] spend the night. . . .

After the game Jerry met April without Sandy.

> [April] said that Sandy had gotten into trouble and was not allowed to stay the night now. . . . I decided to ask what possible mischief Sandy could have gotten into at the game to make her mother change her mind. April said "Her mom's weird sometimes. She said that Sandy should wear a hat and that if she didn't that she couldn't go anywhere after the game."
>
> *Me:* So, did Sandy wear a hat?
> *April:* No.
> *Me:* And you think her mother is strange because she spelled out what she wanted and Sandy balked and faced the consequences?

April: No . . . she was just looking for an excuse to change her mind. . . .

Now, all this time I've been thinking to myself, "Sandy should have worn a hat—it rained all evening and the temperature in the 40's." For that matter, I was wrestling with the idea of should I or should I not get on April's case for not wearing a hat. There she sat, jacket and hair soaked through. But as I reflect back on my own childhood, I can't help but remember how I resented being told all those things by my parents and how they never influenced my actions except maybe by doing the opposite of what they desired.

Me: Well, maybe Sandy's mom felt that she needed a hat. . . . (And I bit my tongue to not say "You needed a hat, dummy, look at you!")
April: She's just weird.
Me: Well, she did know what her mom wanted and the consequences.
April: I know. (pause) I'll tell you, I'm wearing my jacket with my hood the next time.

How often do I respond in the classroom when I should be biting my tongue and practicing patience? I have to wonder about my role (as teacher) as teller. . . . Patience isn't very expedient though, is it?

CREATIVE AND POETIC WRITING

The term *creative* implies for me several characteristics or qualities of mind:

- *Playfulness*, to make light of, to let the mind take off time from conscious directed thought, using one's imagination.
- *Independence and self-confidence*, striking out on one's own, following one's whims.
- *Childlike awareness*, looking at the world from fresh perspectives, as if each flower is the first one beheld, an active engagement in looking and sensing.
- *Openness to experience*, free from defensiveness.
- *Intensity*, energy, the ability to focus energy.
- *Tolerance for ambiguity*, to explore options, flexibility, to withhold judgments, to ponder.
- *Curiosity*, wonder, persistent questioning.

The term *creative* is difficult to define because it is used in many different ways. Here, I'm using it to denote intentionally exploratory writing meant to bring into existence fresh ways of viewing and interpreting life's experiences. Though it can be an exacting and demanding kind of writing, it also entails meandering, surrendering to curiosity, leaving familiar paths. In the journal excerpt that follows, Craig writes playfully—creatively—about a problem that every parent and kindergarten teacher knows only too well.

On Children and Knots

Knots in children's shoes are a complex issue that is very real to many of us. I believe my job as a kindergarten teacher qualifies me as an expert on this subject, and I feel compelled to share my wisdom for the benefit of adulthood everywhere.

There are real knots and pseudo-knots. The distinction can be made with your eyes closed. The more genuine the knot, the wetter it will be from panic-stricken efforts to lick and bite away the snarl. This is unfortunate since adults were clearly given better teeth than children so we could more effectively undo even the most savage knots. However, few of us can really force ourselves to be the second licker on a knot, and thus, we become ineffective in the eyes of our children.

The best way to handle pseudo-knots offered as bids for attention is to protest frustration and reach for the scissors. A miraculous display of self-help is made by the child, and the problem is solved. It is best to not try to be even the first licker on these knots.

Knots result from a variety of circumstances. Basically, kids' shoelaces, like their pencils, are either too long or too short. Too long laces encourage adults to double and triple-tie shoes, presenting an attraction powerful enough to rival Popeye. A few minutes with this marvelous toy, and we are facing a very wet knot.

On the other hand, laces too short in the hands of the child enamored of new-found tying skill result in the most insidious form of knot, the kind with no visible handles. Children fail to recognize the gravity of this situation, and the saliva runs freely.

Adults would do well to attend to this very real problem. Anyone who can solve it will have the undying gratitude of everyone from teachers to Grandma. Do we ever really blame a particularly tricky knot for being late, even if it is the truth?

As Kate prepares for the start of a new school year she writes about what it might be like to be a child on the very first day of school. It provides her with a fresh and useful way to understand first-day anxieties.

Monday, Sept. 7th.
I went to see my kindergarten teacher today. When we got to school, my mom seemed as scared as I did—she didn't know what to do either.

There were other moms and kids in the room. The teacher had my mom sit down at a little table and write on some papers. She told me to find my name tag. I was scared that I couldn't, but I did. I pinned it on all by myself. One of the other kids couldn't do it.

The teacher said to sit down on the green rug—I thought we would sit at desks like my brother does in second grade. We sang a song after the teacher sang it. It was sort of hard to remember the words, but she said we were good. We counted all the kids— It was easy—I can count more than 6!

When the teacher took us over to the door I got sort of scared, but she just showed us the bus on the door and how to find our room. Then we went out and she shut the door to show us the bus on the other side. I knew my mom was still in there, so it was o.k. We went down to see where the buses come in, and then we had to find our room again. I was glad I knew which way to turn!

When we got back to the room the moms were still there writing. I felt a little better. Maybe school won't be so scary after all!

Many journal and diary writers write lyrically. It can be spontaneous, stream-of-consciousness writing that may evolve into deliberate, polished prose.

My journal contains many entries that look like poetry. It isn't poetry by intent; it is the way words come out most naturally sometimes. For me, creative or lyrical writing is a chance to rest my conscious mind and to let what I know but don't know that I know break through into words. Sometimes the force of an idea is surprisingly strong, the vividness and poignancy of images suggesting that we experience more than we realize. Sometimes the words just pour forth with their own line and rhythm, as one stormy spring day these did. I stood looking from a second-story window onto a wooded lot below where a small clump of yellow peeked through damp gray-brown leaves.

one goddamn daffodil
alone
in a forest
  not a forest of beauty
    and growth
  a forest
  in decline
  oaks and maples
  tulip trees split
  crashed and fallen
    through violent winds
    lightning
    thunder storms
  uprooted fallen strength
years of growing
slumber and shade
Trees
which held the hands of
  countless nests
birds in and out of town
and
life;
beheld dramas
through the years
and through a drama felled
The forest now is
chaos
now in decline
The sturdy trees are all but gone
their day is over
now the forest ground supports
  young fast growing trees
which reproduce like cancer
choking out the old
  not letting anything
  encroach
Except that one damned daffodil

THE SEARCH

There are many ways that the journal can help the author make sense of
experience. Writing is an antidote to the anesthetic that slowly be-
clouds us as we step into routines that protect us from the many de-

mands of teaching. As Maxine Greene (1982) points out, "persons must be aroused to self-reflectiveness; they must be moved to search," to wide-awakeness (6).

The search is an age-old inquiry into what it means to be human. Who am I? Why am I here? What is life? Knowing oneself is a humbling process; and wisdom is a lifelong pursuit, as Alice Walker so poignantly sets out in *The Color Purple* (1982):

> Anyhow, he say, you know how it is. You ast yourself one question, it lead to fifteen. I start to wonder why us need love. Why us suffer. Why us black. Why us men and women. Where do children really come from. It didn't take long to realize I didn't hardly know nothing. And that if you ast yourself why you black or a man or a woman or a bush it don't mean nothing if you don't ast why you here, period.
>
> So what you think? I ast.
>
> I think us here to wonder, myself. To wonder. To ast. And that in wondering bout the big things and asting bout the big things, you learn about the little ones, almost by accident. But you never know nothing more about the big things than you start out with. . . . (247)

PART TWO

Keeping a Journal: Exploring Personal and Professional Development

Travelling outward and inward at the same time is less a matter of physical impossibility than a condition of mental health and moral well-being.

Thomas Mallon

In 1969, Joseph Schwab declared (to the consternation of many curricularists) that curriculum as a field was moribund. He argued that the dominant technical, behavioristic paradigm, which he labeled "theoretic," was impractical. The "teacher-proof curriculum," designed in many cases by specialists outside the field of education, was not only an insult to teachers, it was an evasion of responsibility by educators. The rush to outside experts (psychologists and subject matter specialists), he felt, too often ended in flight into "discourse about the field instead of action that resolves problems" (in Schubert 1986, 173–74). Schwab was more concerned with *how* curriculum inquiry should proceed than with *what* the curriculum should be. His concern was shared by other educators, though many took issue with his claim that curriculum as a field was dying.

The next decade witnessed significant strides in practical inquiry. Lawrence Stenhouse and his colleagues from the Centre for Applied Research in Education in East Anglia, John Elliott and others at the Cambridge Institute of Education, along with educators at the Schools Council and those working under the auspices of the Nuffield Foundation, engaged in pioneering efforts at collaborative research within schools in England. In the United States, the Curriculum Reconceptualists came into being. They represented many different perspectives on teaching, research, and curriculum development but joined together in their discontent with the reigning empirical-analytical paradigm (Schubert 1986). Maxine Greene (1973), from an existential-philosophical perspective, suggested that teachers must be moved to be "wide awake," to approach teaching as "strangers" who continuously make decisions to create their worlds; William Pinar (1980, 1981) and Madeline Grumet (1980) explored personal, autobiographical, and life history dimensions of teaching and teachers; Dwayne Huebner (1975) and others (MacDonald & Leeper 1966) inquired into the language and metaphors of educational practice and discourse.

Technological images of schooling, of teachers as writers of behavioral objectives and conveyors of knowledge slowly gave way to more humane conceptions of schooling and teachers whose responsibilities were practical and dynamic. In *An Introduction to Curriculum Research and Development* (1975), Stenhouse wrote of "the Teacher as Researcher":

[C]urriculum research and development ought to belong to the teacher . . . there are prospects of making this good in practice. I concede that it will require a generation of work, and if the majority of teachers—rather than only the enthusiastic few—are to possess this field of research, that the teacher's professional self-image and conditions of work will have to change. (142)

During the 1970s and 1980s the shift was gradually from research *on* classrooms to research *in* classrooms and finally to research *with* teachers and *by* teachers. Stenhouse's "teacher as researcher" has come to be the model toward which many educators direct their efforts. At the same time, there has been research on how teachers conceptualize and think about teaching, their decision making and mental constructs, their philosophical orientations and assumptions. Though the dominant trend is still research on teachers' teaching, there is movement toward teacher inquiry and research. Journal writing furthers this teacher inquiry and research.

From Schwab's call for the practical to Stenhouse's researching teacher, we have come to Donald Schön's "reflective practitioner." Building in part

Keeping a
Exploring
and Profes
Developm

Travelling outward and inwa
time is less a matter of phy
bility than a condition of men
moral well-being.

T

In 1969, Joseph Schwab declared (to the const
ularists) that curriculum as a field was moribu
dominant technical, behavioristic paradigm, whi
was impractical. The "teacher-proof curriculum,
by specialists outside the field of education, wa
teachers, it was an evasion of responsibility by
outside experts (psychologists and subject matter
often ended in flight into "discourse about the fie
resolves problems" (in Schubert 1986, 173–74).
cerned with *how* curriculum inquiry should proc
curriculum should be. His concern was shared by
many took issue with his claim that curriculum

on Polanyi's concept of tacit knowledge—that we know more than we can say—Schön (1983) describes how practitioners inquire naturally in the process of teaching:

> The practitioners' hypothesis-testing experiment is a game with the situation. They seek to make the situation conform to their hypothesis but remain open to the possibility that it will not. Thus their hypothesis-testing activity is neither self-fulfilling prophesy, which insures against the apprehensions of disconfirming data, nor is it the neutral hypothesis testing of the method of controlled experiment, which calls for the experimentor to avoid influencing the object of study and to embrace disconfirming data. The practice situation is neither clay to be molded at will nor an independent, self-sufficient object of study from which the inquirer keeps his distance.
>
> The inquirer's relation to this situation is transactional. He shapes the situation, but in conversation with it, so that his own models and appreciations are also shaped by the situation. The phenomena that he seeks to understand are partly of his own making; he is *in* the situation that he seeks to understand.
>
> . . . The action by which he tests his hypothesis is also a move by which he tries to effect a desired change in the situation, and a probe by which he explores it. He understands the situation by trying to change it. . . . (150–51)

Rather than the isolated professional who is taught to maintain an air of certainty, Schön's practitioner reveals uncertainties.

> He gives up the rewards of unquestioned authority, the freedom of practice without challenge to his competence, the comfort of relative invulnerability, the gratification of deference. The new satisfactions open to him are largely those of discovery—about the meanings of his advice to clients, about his knowledge-in-practice, and about himself. When practice is a repetitive administration of techniques to the same kind of problems, the practitioner may look to leisure as a source of relief, or to early retirement; but when he functions as a researcher-in-practice, the practice itself is a source of renewal. The recognition of error, with its resulting uncertainty, can become a source of discovery rather than an occasion for self-defense. (298)

Although there are no guaranteed approaches either to research into practice or to building the kind of professional environment that supports continuous development, there are several ways in which writing can contribute to these evolving processes. In Part One we explored different kinds of personal documents and writing. In Part Two journal writing and professional practice coalesce; journal writing becomes a tool for the search. Here, journal writing and collegial discussion are portrayed as unique tools for educators, ones that enable them to define and practice professional education. Chapter 8 is designed for getting started in journal writing. Chapter 9 addresses writing about classroom life through vignettes and portraits and discusses portraiture as an educational process. Chapters 10 and 11 present methods of inquiry for exploring personal and professional dimensions of practice. The concluding chapter summarizes ways in which the journal writer can reflect on writing and learn from practice.

SECTION IV

*Practical Suggestions
for Writing about
Experience*

What fun it is to generalize in the privacy
of a notebook. It is as I imagine waltzing
on ice might be. A great delicious sweep in
one direction, taking you your full strength,
and then with no trouble at all, an equally
delicious sweep in the opposite direction. . . .

Florida Scott-Maxwell

Here is where documenting the real-life adventures of teaching begins,
with the intent to write about practice. Chapter 8, "Getting Started,"
should do just that: get you going in ways that will help you enjoy and
learn from first writings. In chapter 9, "Life on Paper," examples are
drawn from educators' and writers' work in constructing vignettes and
portraits of practice—the here-and-now that constitutes the evolving stories of professional life.

CHAPTER 8

Getting Started

"Where shall I begin, please your Majesty?" he asked. "Begin at the beginning," the king said, gravely, "and go on till you come to the end: then stop."

Lewis Carroll

MATERIALS FOR WRITING

You'll first need to select materials for writing. Although this may not seem to be an important consideration—we are accustomed to scribbling on whatever is available at the moment—it's wise to give some thought to materials that will make it more comfortable to write over a long period of time. Simons (1978) suggests that durability, size, and flexibility be considered. I'll add a fourth consideration: personal preference.

Where you intend to write will make a difference in the size journal you select. If you intend to carry it with you, your journal will need to be durable and small enough to transport comfortably. Yet smaller journals aren't particularly easy to write in. Stenographer pads, designed to be carried, also have the benefit of wire loops for quick opening and a flat surface for writing. I've found, though, that pages tear out too readily, that it's easy to become confused from entry to entry about which way the pages run, and that they truly are designed for shorthand: there isn't all that much room to write sentence-length entries. Large notebooks or journal pads are easier to write in, but they're bulky.

Both small and large books for journal keeping are available in stationery stores and book shops. Some are made with fairly high-quality paper and have attractive and durable board covers. Bound books have the advantage of keeping all of the writing together in one place, and, because of their permanent format, they dissuade the writer from tearing out pages (which at the moment may seem better thrown out, but later might be viewed quite differently). Loose-leaf notebooks don't appear quite so professional, nor is the quality of paper necessarily as good. They have the advantage of flexibility, though. Pages can be removed (don't throw them away!) and sections reorganized as ideas are developed. Another plus is that loose-leaf binders open flat, which makes for a stable writing surface. Book-type journals are by comparison difficult to write in. I find it most convenient to keep a regular-sized loose-leaf notebook and to either write on standard, lined paper or punch holes in whatever other paper is available at the time. This gives me the opportunity to write wherever and whenever I choose and later insert the page(s) in the journal. I also carry a small, bound pocket journal, which usually gets filled within a month or two.

Many of us find it useful to carry on a dialogue between different parts of our journals. Progoff (1975), for example, recommends keeping several sections in the journal to allow momentum and energy to develop as a result of interactive dialogue among the different sections. His divisions include a historical section, a daily log, a section for dreams, and several others. It's well worth your considering such a format, not necessarily designed around Progoff's divisions but those that promise to work for you.

For journal writing, try selecting a pen or pencil that fits your mood. You might also try writing with more than one color. At times, red might suit the subject; at other times, blue or green. Another way to use color is to differentiate one day from the next so that you can see quickly where an entry begins and ends. It can also be useful to use a different color pen to make marginal comments when you reread your journal. (Note the marginalia in Figure 8–1, excerpted pages from one of my pocket journals.) An alternative is double-spacing, which allows for the interlinear addition of comments.

JOURNAL WRITING WITH A WORD PROCESSOR

William Zinsser (1983) suggests that a person can learn enough to use a word processor to begin writing in about ten minutes. It took me twenty. From then on I learned as I went along. Journal writing with a word processor is different in several ways from writing on paper. It is faster and easier by far than writing longhand, and the results are easier to read. A word processor is more flexible than a typewriter. Mistakes can be corrected quickly, additions inserted anywhere, and deletions made in scant seconds. Entire passages can be moved and regrouped. For example, it would be a simple operation to gather all pertinent entries about a particular student or a project together into a single file, no matter how

FIGURE 8–1

Pocket Journal Excerpt with Marginalia

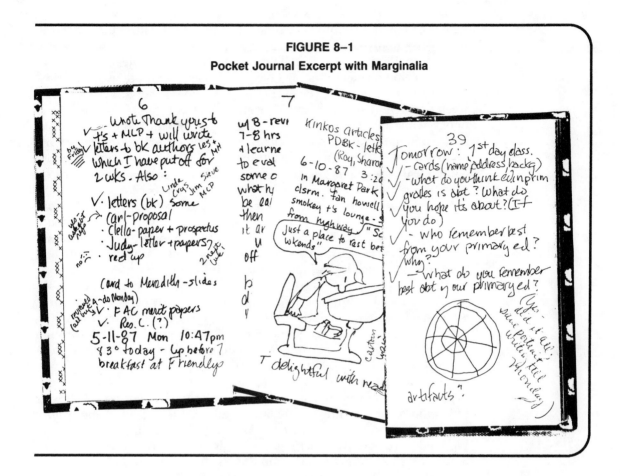

many entries or how much time they span. This is particularly useful when working on a case study or compiling a profile over time.

But no, you don't *need* a word processor; they are a great convenience, even a pleasure. In no journal-keeping circumstance I can think of, however, is such a device essential.

TIMES AND PLACES TO WRITE

Removing ourselves from the busyness of our professional lives long enough to write about them is no small task. When should you write, and for how long? Evenings, mornings, weekends? How important is time for reflection? Thirty minutes a day? Two hours a week? Four? Seven?

Plan time for writing into your schedule, at least until it becomes a habit, which eventually it will.

If at first writing seems to be time-consuming, take heart. Your writing can help you save time by helping you become more aware of how you use it. One teacher, for example, kept a log of her activities over a week and found that she spent several hours correcting student workbooks while lamenting that she didn't have enough time for creative writing. Students didn't seem to learn from her corrections, nor did many seem to make good use of their time while waiting for classmates to complete their work. Using her log to identify problems and reflecting on possible solutions, she decided to begin the class period with creative writing and to have the students complete and grade their own workbooks either after they finished their creative writing or when they needed a break. As a result, she found that they were much more enthusiastic about writing and were learning to pace themselves and to profit from their mistakes; and that she had more time to give individual attention to their writing.

There are three time periods to consider for writing in your journal. Sometimes you'll write about an experience *before it occurs*, perhaps to plan a new lesson or organize the day. Use your journal to think through what, how, and why you are going to do something and what the consequences may be.

Another optimum time to record is *as close to the time of the experience as possible*. Usually the writing will consist of a few key words and phrases to help in reconstructing events later. The third time for writing is *after the experience occurs*—according to Progoff (1975), the sooner the better. We tend to remember experiences selectively, and the closer in time to the occurrence we note them, the less likely we are to omit or change important details. In other instances, some distancing may be beneficial.

Many people find a quiet time at night to think back over events they then record. Some teachers sit down at school, after the students leave, to write about events that took place that day (see, for example, Figure 1–1). They find it easier to recall and visualize what happened in the classroom by writing there. Other teachers write brief journal entries when time is available throughout the week. (One professor I know jots while standing in bank lines, sitting in the doctor's waiting room, and even waiting in a grocery check-out line.) Some teachers, like Marcy, set aside time during the school day for journal writing—their own and their students'. She leaves her journal open on her desk so that the students may read it if they wish. Both Marcy and they select writing to share.

Whenever you choose to write, it is important that you allocate sufficient time to reflect quietly. This means time away from all other demands. According to Progoff (1975), we need a quiet setting where we can contemplate while the tensions of the day recede. Where you write might also depend on what you write. Craig leaves his journal on his desk and makes jottings throughout the day, which he then expands on at night. On Sunday evenings he sets aside an hour or two for reflection and writing on topics of special interest. Judy writes a few days a week either before or after school for short stretches and then relaxes on Friday evenings with a glass of wine, a pencil, and paper (sometimes she describes events; other times she works out concerns or cogitates introspectively; and sometimes she plays with ideas). You might find that for descriptive writing, quiet isn't necessary, while for reflective, introspective writing, it is.

You won't always write even though you have planned to. You might go for days, weeks, or longer without writing. I used to feel guilty about this. But it seemed that the more guilt I felt, the less willing I was to take up the pen again—even when I really wanted to write! Once I stopped wringing my hands, I realized that every day didn't have to be recorded, and I began to write again. Now, I resume when it seems appropriate and make notes of important occurrences since I last wrote. Nor do I try to include as much. It is often more useful to be highly selective when reconstructing experiences. (Does it really matter that Danny's mother wore a purple hat when she picked him up at school?) So, I summarize or highlight a few significant events and ideas and move on to more current experiences. Sylvia Ashton-Warner summarized over time by noting events of most personal significance, focusing, for example, on one classroom event in reading and writing rather than writing more generally about several.

Like the human development that writing mirrors, there are cycles in journal keeping. At times it seems very important to write; at other times it might be equally important not to. There are times when we are too close to an experience to face reflecting on it in writing. A few days later, though, it could be highly beneficial.

GETTING STARTED

"Where shall I begin, please . . . ?" With the date. Date everything. And even if you begin not knowing what you will write about, try titling each piece before you finish writing for the day. Since much that we write about seems mundane, it might not seem important to record the date. But it is these ordinary events, as well as extraordinary experiences, that define life; and at the time of their occurrence, we often cannot tell which is which. Dating and assigning titles to journal entries also makes it possible to rearrange writing under new section headings if this becomes appropriate.

Of the many ways to begin journal writing, freewriting and autobiographical writing are two of the easiest, most enjoyable and productive.

Freewriting

According to Peter Elbow (1973) freewriting is sometimes called "automatic writing," "babbling," or "jabbering."

> The idea is simply to write for ten minutes (later on, perhaps fifteen or twenty). Don't stop for anything. Go quickly without rushing. Never stop to look back, to cross something out, to wonder how to spell something, to wonder what word or thought to use, or to think of what you are doing. . . . The easiest thing is just to put down whatever is in your mind. . . . (3)

He recommends that this type of writing not be evaluated or judged in any way. The purpose is to write without editing, to allow thoughts to flow unrestrictedly onto the page. Instead of worrying about how our writing will sound, we almost trick ourselves into writing about what has meaning to us, much as we do when we talk without much conscious thought. Elbow (1973) describes such a circumstance:

> [T]he words he produces have this striking integration or coherence: he isn't having to plan and work them out one by one. They are all permeated by his meaning. . . . Not merely manipulated by his mind, but rather, sifted through his entire self. In such writing you don't feel mechanical cranking, you don't hear the gears change. . . .
> . . . If you do freewriting regularly, much or most of it will be inferior to what you can produce through care and rewriting. But the *good* bits will be much better than anything else you can produce by any other method. (8–9)

Freewriting regularly (Elbow suggests three times a week) generates topics to write on. For example, some journal writers have found that freewriting limbers them up for writing and that after they have completed this as an exercise, they pull out an idea or phrase to write about in a more thoughtful manner. Freewriting about whatever events return to mind at the end of a day is a useful way to discover worthwhile topics for journal writing. Begin by listing three or four possible topics: Jane's poem, lunchtime talk, recess duty, problems with a new student. Now select one of these topics and write nonstop on it for ten or fifteen minutes. After freewriting, sit back and read what you have written. Simply "look to see what words or passages seemed important—attracted energy or strength. Here is your cue what to write" (Elbow 1973, 9). Freewriting can be an exhilarating experience, both as you learn to look forward to the time to do it, and as you document the development of your journey—personally and professionally.

Autobiographical Writing

A short autobiography can provide a fitting beginning to your journal. Start with the evolving story that you will continue to explore and create as long as you write. You might wish to designate a section of your journal for autobiographical writing.

Writing autobiographically can grow out of freewriting or it can be done in conjunction with it. In either case it can help you to locate yourself in the context of development—to get a sense of your history. Like Jerry, who wrote autobiographically in short entries throughout his journal, you will find this type of writing can lead to insights and self-understanding. You might respond to these sorts of questions:

- Why did you become a teacher?
- When and how did you decide?
- What and who influenced you?
- In what ways?
- As you look back, possibly to your first years of schooling, what feelings and images remain?
- Which teachers do you remember, and why do you remember them?
- What do you remember about them?
- Focus on one or two teachers who really influenced you. What adjectives might you use to describe them?
- What were the most meaningful aspects of your education (including teacher education) that contributed to your development as a teacher?
- If you could make the decision again to become a teacher (or administrator), would you? Why or why not? Did you consider other options?
- In what ways does teaching fit with values relating to education in your home?
- What are other family members' attitudes toward your work? How might these influence you?
- Why do you continue to be an educator?

As you begin your journal, pose questions to yourself. Write in response to some questions, and leave others for later entries. How you proceed to use your journal will depend on your reasons for writing; but autobiographical writing, whether given a section of your journal or integrated throughout it, can be a rewarding and useful kind of writing. It includes reflective, introspective, and descriptive writing and is therapeutic. It provides an evolving basis for interpreting and understanding yourself as an educator.

FIGURE 8–2
Journal Excerpt—Carole

1. Monica hospitalized. → problems

2.

32. Attended rally in Cols. joys

3. - Interactions affected teaching

4. What setting

5. What have I changed.

I - Monica hospitalized - Suely had bruises on her bottom. Davey caught stealing cookies at Lawsons before school - parents are starting to question me about 2nd grade Placement → Racial problems at the high school Gave Iowa based tests - some did not do well.

"Regular" Writing

Some teachers find it useful to begin by sitting down at the end of the day and recalling thoughts, feelings, and meaningful incidents. They begin by jotting down ideas to write about and then expand on a few. Figure 8–2 is such an excerpt from Carole's journal.

It might be easier to write about your experiences and plans if you talk about them first, either to yourself or with a colleague. Some people

FIGURE 8–2
(continued)

I. Attended rally in Cols. for state funding. (4)
Appointed program Chairperson for KEA involves (4)
inservice day. Students are starting to
really express their feelings about me as they (1)
realize that the year is ending and they will be
going on. Much affection has been shown. Parents are (1)
getting involved in the classroom sharing their affection.
III Got involved with Monica situation. My
feelings about what has happened to her made
me question whether or not we did everything (2)
we should have. Got involved with school
funding.
IV- The interaction took place in the hospital, on (3)
the phone with social workers & doctors.
V- I've changed my answer to parents concerning
~~whether or not~~ to placement for their
child in second grade. I used to tell them
that I would see what I can do. I am
now putting the problem on my principal (9)
and telling them that they must request
a certain teacher by talking or writing to
the principal. I've also changed my
feelings about what responsibility the school
has in intervening when ~~the~~ a child is being
neglected or abused.

find it helpful to talk into a tape recorder, by themselves or with a colleague. They play the tape back and stop it at times to write. This, in fact, is how the monograph *Keeping a Personal-Professional Journal* (Holly 1983) came into being.

Logs

The log-type journal entry forms in Figures 8–3 and 8–4 were developed to provide some structure for beginning journal keepers. Similar logs have also been useful for experienced teachers. These are meant to serve as general models; you should design your own log sheets around your own concerns.

Some teachers find it useful at the beginning of a month or term to put a calendar in their journals and note long-range plans and upcoming events. Having in mind what is coming lends a deepened sense of direction to activities and teaching. Preparation enables flexibility and the chance to seize unusual opportunities because we don't have to be preoccupied with what to do next. Hence, we increase our options. If I know that I want students to study their town and prepare to share their work with others the following month during the Community Festival, I can plan several activities (invite local historians in to speak, take a field trip to the museum, interview government officials, etc.) and then take advantage of the possibilities as they present themselves. In the weekly log I'll record what we do as we do it.

Information relative to students and to teaching is often more consciously addressed in a log than in a plan book. The former can be invaluable in this respect, mainly because a log invites the writer to move past standard fill-in-the-blanks planning. Indeed, an intermediate step toward keeping a professional log is to make reflective notes in the margins of your current plan book at those junctures where the plans deal with the subjects that figure in your reflective notes. (Logs also offer the advantage of privacy, in itself an incentive to reflect and write freely.)

TOPICS

You can write about anything. Topics and experiences are as diverse as your imagination. Document your thoughts, feelings, plans, descriptions, analyses, and introspection as you explore teaching and professional development. Focus your writing on each of several dimensions of your professional life including: (1) you as an educator, past, present, and future (why you do what you do); (2) students—descriptions of their behavior, its contexts, your responses to it; (3) collegial interactions; and

FIGURE 8–3

Weekly Log

Schedule of special activities this week:
Monday:

Tuesday:

Wednesday:

Thursday:

Friday:

Things I must accomplish:

Things I want to accomplish:

Need special attention (students, activities):

Things to remember:

Comments and review; looking ahead:

FIGURE 8–4
Daily Log

Plan:

Most important events/happenings:

Comments on students:

Comments on teaching/learning:

Tomorrow:

(4) the processes of professional development—your thoughts as you plan, reflect on, and explore teaching and professional development.

You as an Educator

In addition to the questions posed above, in the section "Autobiographical Writing" (and those suggested in chapter 10), consider the following:

- How would you describe yourself as an educator?
- How might you like others to describe you as an educator?
- How would you describe your roles and responsibilities?
- What do you know about your styles of working?
- About interacting with others?
- What do you consider to be your strengths as an educator? Your weaknesses?
- If you were not an educator, what might you do?
- What and who influences your work?
- What are the biggest challenges you face? the biggest frustrations? the greatest joys and satisfactions?
- What hopes do you have for the children you teach?
- What patterns can you identify in your teaching?
- What aspects of your work might benefit from more focused attention?
- What might you be doing two (or five, or fifteen) years from now?

Students

Daily jottings about students, as well as vignettes, portraits, and case studies, can provide useful information for teaching. Include information not only about the students but also about yourself and your interactions with students.

- How would you describe the students with whom you work?
- What do you know about the students you teach?
- Which students are you particularly concerned about? Why?
- Might it be helpful to concentrate on your work with a student or group over time, documenting and discussing the process of working with them?
- What kinds of short, descriptive comments entered in your journal over time might enable you to better understand a student?

Professional Interactions

Your professional interactions can also be a source of ideas:

- With whom do you interact professionally?
- Do you consider them to be colleagues (as opposed to fellow staff members, for example)? Why?

- What are your most important interactions and communications during the day or week? Significant curriculum development? Staff development?
- In what ways might curriculum and staff development be related?
- How would you describe your interactions with parents, administrators, other staff members? Other educators and community members outside the school?

Professional Development and Writing

Then there are questions related to your own environment:

- What are the social, economic, political, and historical contexts within which you teach?
- What do you know or can you find out about the history of the community and schools where you teach? where you attended school?
- How do these contexts influence your work?
- How do you feel about sharing your writing about teaching and professional development with a colleague or colleagues?

Over time you will connect writing in different dimensions of your professional life as relationships emerge. The extent to which you are able to describe your relationship to the circumstances and actions in your journal will in part determine what you can learn from them.

TWO GENERAL SUGGESTIONS ABOUT JOURNAL WRITING

Two general suggestions to keep in mind have been alluded to already: relax, and write vividly.

Relax

Though you will not always be relaxed when you write, it is important that you often are, especially as you begin to write regularly. Relax and let the motion of the day subside; let an inner peace take over. Protect a time and place that are yours, where you can feel yourself unwind. Few occupations are as physically, emotionally, socially, and intellectually demanding as teaching is. Take a few minutes to allow your breathing to become deeper and slower. This sets the tone for reflective writing. Jerry finds it useful to weave himself into music, to let the past and the future fade as the present comes into focus. Regardless of how you remove yourself from outward action, the important point is that you do so.

Write Vividly

When recording experiences, describe them as vividly as possible. Include as much detail as you need to convey the occurence and your responses to it. As you gain facility in writing, you will probably enjoy the challenges of translating your experiences into words and of recapturing the circumstances. But beware: what you have recorded is only a likeness of reality—it is not the reality itself. Reality moves; it is in a constant state of flux. When you write, keep in mind the transitory nature of your reconstructions. Words (like theories) are partial pictures derived from experience at specific times—segments of a flowing process.

Although we are never able to actually return to our experiences, it is helpful to describe them as vividly as we can so that the images we retain will be as close as possible to meaningful dimensions of the experiences. This is what Eudora Welty (1983) meant when she wrote of searching for truth in her words: it means using all of our senses—as we did when we were children.

> Children, like animals, use all their senses to discover the world. Then artists come along and discover it the same way, all over again. Here and there, it's the same world. Or now and then we'll hear from an artist who's never lost it.
>
> In my sensory education I include my physical awareness of the *word*. Of a certain word, that is; the connection it has with what it stands for. At around age six, perhaps, I was standing by myself in our front yard waiting for supper, just at that hour in a late summer day when the sun is already below the horizon and the risen full moon in the visible sky stops being chalky and begins to take on light. There comes the moment, and I saw it then, when the moon goes from flat to round. For the first time it met my eyes as a globe. The word "moon" came into my mouth as though fed to me out of a silver spoon. Held in my mouth the moon became a word. It had the roundness of a Concord grape Grandpa took off his vine and gave me to suck out its skin and swallow whole, in Ohio. (10)

CHAPTER 9

Life on Paper:
Vignettes and Portraits

> Such fast and intuitive work could never be characterized as classical, systematic research; . . . our written pieces would reveal at least as much about the authors as they did about the school settings. . . . I suggested we call our pieces "portraits." . . .
>
> *Sarah Lawrence Lightfoot*

VIGNETTES

A vignette is a short sketch or picture. It can be of people, events, or personal experiences. Vignettes reflect the many voices of the writer. They sometimes show the writer's emotion, as does this excerpt, taken from an elementary school principal's journal:

> The lights went out. All the kids got quiet. I was concerned. They hadn't been very noisy. Why was the light out? Because Mr. B. says they are to be quiet for a week cause they were bad. Shit. A whole week. They were bad cause they weren't supervised. We screw up and they suffer. I ranted and raved and told some teachers off. Of course I had to back them. That's what really hurt. I told them that . . . [t]his isn't a Gestapo Camp!

Jim, this elementary school principal, writes regularly in his journal in the form of vignettes. The following was written after a teacher left his office with a problem for which he has no solution. By the time he finishes writing about the incident (and reflecting on others that morning), he knows he is writing about many people, including himself:

The teacher comes in and her problem is super important. She tries to tell you and you actually do understand—the trouble is that you have heard of 5–6 other super problems already and you somehow can't get as panicked as she wants. "Do your best" doesn't work with her.

Teachers also want answers that aren't there.

Vignettes are small literary sketches of life that often fade gradually into larger pictures; they are segments that begin a story, and they are the smaller stories within a story: small centers of interest within a landscape or a painting or a life. They can also stand by themselves. They are glimmers of action: past teaching and educational experiences, current pictures of political life, daily events. Life histories are composed of biographical or autobiographical vignettes, segments of experience that, when integrated, form patterns and themes. They make it possible to identify developmental progressions and change, and they provide the substance for the construction of portraits.

PORTRAITS

A portrait is a likeness. It can be of a person, place, time, event, or circumstance. It is a depiction in words, a graphic representation which reveals both more and less of the reality it symbolizes. The portraitist takes liberties and artistic license to create the sense or essence of the subject.

The essential thrust is toward a reasonably accessible and suggestive "reading" of a given person's life. The writers become mediators; through them another life reaches toward the reader, and if the work has been successful, stays with the reader as a guest, a "spirit," whose mind and heart and soul have been registered upon the consciousness of distant strangers. (Coles & Coles 1980, 4)

In constructing a portrait, the author writes biographically or autobiographically, but usually not with the intention of compiling a full-fledged biography. The term *biography* implies a more detailed and comprehensive accounting of a person's life. Although a well-written biography may be a work of art, it generally resembles a photographic essay or film more than it does a painting.

> A fine biography is first of all a work of scholarship, grounded in the virtues of diligent and scrupulous research, judicious evaluation of information, and a fresh vision of connections between persons, places, and events. (Horner, in Coles & Coles 1980, xi)

In writing a portrait, the author tries to capture the insider's view of what is important and in so doing to create a feeling of intimacy with the times and person. Portraits permit us to see the subject in its uniqueness while at the same time connecting it with universal human qualities and circumstances. "The personal dimension of the portraits and their literary, aesthetic qualities create symbols and images that other people can connect with" (Lightfoot 1983, 378). At best, we are taken into the life of another and emerge with understanding, empathy, and ultimately insight into our own being.

While few people construct portraits in the same ways or for the same purposes as Robert Coles and Jane Hallowell Coles, Sarah Lawrence Lightfoot, or other professional writers, there can be significant benefits from more modest attempts. Phenomenological and qualitative methods such as portraiture are particularly valuable in providing broader images of schooling, especially when so much emphasis is placed on measurement and standardized descriptions of educational practice. Through portraiture the educator conveys more of the complexity of interactions and interrelationships involved in teaching and learning than is possible using more linear methods of description. The benefits of portrait construction are many; the process is educative. As the author assembles information, it becomes apparent what is known and what still needs to be ascertained. We begin to make connections. The more we assemble and observe, the more aware we become. The more we structure and write portraits, the more descriptive and facile we become with words.

How are portraits constructed? There are as many ways to write a portrait as there are to create a sculpture or to write a poem.

Brainstorming

Write whatever presents itself in your mind. "Karen had a rough day, not unlike others the last few weeks. . . ." Jot down ideas or themes to include in the portrait: Jason's fears, Maggie's friendships, Marcy's intellectual curiosity, events at faculty meetings. What unique characteristics of the person or circumstance would you like to portray?

To identify characteristics or qualities, jot down plenty of adjectives. You might be surprised when you examine these terms that some appear to contradict one another or to be unsuitable together. I described Carole (chapter 4), for example, as "isolated, collegial, warm, angry, gentle, firm, confident, anxious, distant, troubled, integrated." While I felt very close to her, I felt considerable distance too. I sensed her empathy and sensitivity to children, but also her troubled independence from other teachers, as well as her professional collegiality. Carole, from my perspective, was both distant and collegial. As I tried to give body to the words I generated, I created the portrait. I learned to be more discerning, to look more sensitively at Carole. The adjectives were markers that provided clues for exploring more complex configurations and interactions.

In everyday life in schools we gather many ideas about the people we work with, yet we rarely take the time to integrate these into more comprehensive pictures—to consciously link these ideas to one another. Constructing a portrait is like assembling a puzzle, putting the pieces together so that we see relationships and connections and form a broader picture. In constructing the portraits for the Teacher Reflections project, I tried several methods. I constructed a preliminary portrait by jotting down everything I knew about the person. I expanded these and gathered additional information. "What does a reader need to know?" I asked myself. "Well," I replied, "the point of the study is to look at the teacher's point of view, at how each person looks at teaching and professional development. We need to understand something about Marcy, her background, the contexts within which she teaches, what teaching means to her." From this came general categories: family background, education and schooling experiences, home life and leisure, community and school, professional life, and project participation. I assembled information within each area. Where I needed more information, I contacted the teacher.

For some portraits, I had a friend who didn't know any of the teachers ask me about them. What were they like? What was it like to be in each classroom? What one or two metaphors came to me when I thought about this person? Our conversations were short, but they left me with ideas, which I transferred to 3-by-5-inch index cards. There, in brief, were the portraits. This is also a helpful method for better understanding students. Rather than having someone interview me (though it was valuable), I interview myself. "What do I know about David? In what ways does he contribute to class discussion? When does he seem interested? What possible ways can I build on his experiences, draw him into class discussion?" While it might not be possible to write a portrait for each student, brief ones can be useful for teaching and evaluating. Often, a portrait brings to light information that facilitates working with other students: identifying where difficulties arise in learning, how the person perceives the task of learning, and how teaching might better be structured. Reflecting on students and their learning inevitably takes me back to reflecting on my teaching and professional behavior, ultimately where it can make a difference.

Profiles and Logging Information

Many portraits are constructed from profiles and logs. A profile is an outline of information relative to a person, place, or topic. A classroom profile, for example, might include the number of children, their sexes and ages, attendance, parents' occupations, family size and membership, achievement scores, and any other variables deemed appropriate. A teacher profile, like the ones I kept for the Teacher Reflections study, might include sex, age, level of experience, previous occupations and grade levels taught, administrative and other professional experience, family background and education, professional affiliations and activities, as well as concerns and sources of satisfaction and frustration related to teaching. A profile can contain information drawn from a log. In the case of Teacher Reflections, I had each teacher keep a week's time log of daily interactions outside of regular teaching responsibilities. These then became part of the teacher profiles I compiled.

Student profiles developed over time enable the writer to connect behavior and observations. Connections are more likely to be made when the profile includes information on various aspects of the student's work and interactions. Many academic problems, for example, are related to physical variables. By noting characteristics such as sluggishness or hyperactivity, as well as social interactions, family background, interests, and academic progress, we begin to get a more holistic picture of the child and to see patterns and rhythms in his or her development.

Another benefit in keeping profiles is that patterns across students emerge. A first-year, first-grade teacher, for example, found that several children were not ready developmentally for much of the prescribed curriculum: fine and gross motor control (documented in drawing, painting, printing, and physical education) and social interactions were developmentally different from the other children. At first she worried that she was not teaching well enough, but as she collected information she saw that these differences seemed to hold across many different aspects of life in first grade. While these children's adjustment problems might more quickly be related to developmental characteristics by an experienced teacher, a beginner can use data collection and organizational methods to make sense of what is otherwise an overwhelming confusion of variables: children, schedules, routine, curriculum, time, space, to say nothing about colleagues, staff, parents, and teaching.

Assuming Different Points of View

Construct a portrait of the school from an administrator's perspective: "Portrait of the School Two Years Ago," "Portrait of the School Now," and/or "Portrait of the School Two Years from Now." Answer a letter to the editor of a newspaper or journal by way of a portrait or vignette. Construct a portrait from a child's point of view, or from that of a parent.

In the following excerpts from Craig's journal, he creates portraits of two parents who are about to attend a parent-teacher conference. The community has unusually high unemployment, layoffs from work are common, and the social and educational distance between most teachers and parents is marked. Craig develops two alternative letters. By doing so he brings into focus how parents might feel about meeting with the teacher and how these conferences can influence parent-child relations. He also prepares himself for the conferences. Then, by sharing these letters with other teachers, he initiates collegial discussion.

Dear School Person,

I am writing to you in the middle of the night because I can't sleep. You see, tomorrow I must go for a conference with my son's teacher. Right now I feel bad but it will surely be worse tomorrow night.

There have been years when I looked forward to conferences because the teacher would tell me about the good things my boy does and we could share the excitement of a child we both love. Not this year! I will sit passively and listen to the complaints about my son. Of course, I must believe and trust the teacher; she is wiser than I am; but I won't understand at all and will be afraid to ask. She probably already thinks I am a terrible mother because of the way my boy acts and I wouldn't want to make things any worse by asking dumb questions. So, it won't be a conference at all. More like a lecture. I will get there on time and dress neatly, trying to forget my boss's nasty comment about leaving work early. Surely I can accommodate the teacher who is so busy at such an important job. As I wait patiently while she jokes and laughs with the teacher across the hall, I will tell myself they are talking about something delightful and childlike my boy did today.

My illusion will vanish as she turns and sees me. Her expression will change to grim seriousness and the outwardly friendly greeting will not hide the message she is sending. I will be invited to an uncomfortable chair where I will peer into eyes as cold as the gray steel desk between us. I'll wonder if it is only childhood innocence that allows my son to say he likes this person. Just once I would like to sit at his desk for a conference because that might help me understand how he sees things.

In an effort to occupy my apprehensive imagination, I'll search the room for my boy's dinosaur picture he was so proud of and even called up Grandma to tell her the teacher hung it up in the room. It would make me feel so good if the teacher would point it out, but I know that is not the subject of the conference.

We are going to talk about the papers stacked neatly before the teacher in a folder with my son's name on it. My heart will leap as she opens the folder and there is a very complicated-looking paper on the top with a big smiley face on it. Maybe it will be different this time I'll hope. But in a flash, that paper is turned down and one covered with red slashes appears and I know my worst fears are going to be realized. For the next twenty minutes I will stare at red ink and listen to a catalog of my son's deficiencies. I'll draw attention to good papers and even correct answers on the bad ones but I'll be made to feel I'm interrupting. I'll search in vain again for the dinosaur picture.

Of course, I will ask how I can help my son at home but I will not get an answer that means anything to me. The teacher seems to feel I won't help or that I'm too dumb to help him learn school things. She is, I think, afraid that I might teach him something that she couldn't.

Next she will ask me if there is anything I want to talk about but that is only her way of telling me the conference is over. I'll think again of the dinosaur picture, or perhaps of the drawer of bills at home, my husband's impending lay-off, the leaky roof, or my father ill in the rest home or the full day of household chores awaiting me at the end of work. I'll say, "No, I think we've covered it. Thank you for your time."

The four blocks home will seem like miles because of my depression. My son is doing badly in school! When I get home I will yell at my boy about his work, take away his bicycle and unplug the TV. He'll ask if I liked his dinosaur picture.

A little while later my son will come down into the kitchen and ask "Mom, why are you crying?" I won't be able to answer but I'll think, "Son, if your teacher makes you feel bad like she made me feel, I understand why you have trouble."

A parent

Dear School Person,

It's really late at night and I can't sleep so I decided to write to you. Tomorrow I go for a conference with my son's teacher and I'm so excited. I'm anticipating a wonderful and rewarding meeting and being on top of the world tomorrow night.

There have been years when conferences were awful experiences and I heard about a child I didn't even know. Not this year!

I am trying to think of all the things I want to tell my child's teacher; she is always so interested in me. That says she really cares about my boy. She always makes a point to comment on the good job I've done raising my pride and joy and I would never hesitate to ask her advice on anything. Sometimes conferences with her are difficult because I do most of the talking and I'm really a quiet person.

I might be a little late and my dress mussed a trifle but I know the teacher won't mind. She knows I work hard all day and she appreciates my effort to come. Once when I was talking to her the principal asked to see her and she told him she didn't have time right then. That made me feel important.

I always feel silly sitting at my child's desk for conferences but it helps me share the energy and excitement he feels about school. His teacher sits there with me and I think that this is a person just like me with a hard job, housework, and kids of her own. I'll even bet her son gets in the same mischief as mine.

Tomorrow we will just sit down when we'll have to jump up to look at my son's dinosaur picture hanging on the bulletin board. She'll chuckle when I tell her of the exuberant call to Grandma about it.

Then we'll sit back down and start looking at my boy's work. I can see there are lots of problems with it and I'm concerned. Since I don't know very much about school and kid's learning, the teacher will carefully explain the progress my son is making and show me examples of how he is learning from his mistakes. We'll spend a long time on a hard paper with a big smiley face on it and the teacher won't let me get caught up talking about my son's wrong answers. She wants to talk about the right ones.

I'll say I'll be glad to work with my son at home and she says she knows I already do that. How does she know? But she'll go to her desk and get some materials she has made herself and suggest my son might like to work on them with me. She might even give me a copy of my son's reader in a brown bag with the caution, "Don't tell anyone I gave you this."

I'll know the conference is getting to the really important part when she asks if there is anything I want to talk about. I feel so open with her. I'll talk about the pressures at home with my husband being laid off and all. She says she will keep her ears open for a job and I'll know she means it. We'll talk about the housework and how hard it is to have a job and not feel guilty about being a neglectful mother. She'll remember my father in the rest home and sincerely ask about him. I'll be so flattered.

We'll part as friends. I'll come home in a flash, dancing through the door with hugs and kisses for my son. He'll ask about the dinosaur picture and I'll tell him that the shade of purple he picked for the tail was just right and that he is terrific.

A little while later, my son will find me in the kitchen laughing to myself. "Why?" he'll ask. I'll hug him and answer "I was thinking how much I would like to go to your class everyday, just like you do."

A parent

ETHICAL AND PROFESSIONAL CONSIDERATIONS IN LIFE WRITING

As with any personal document, writing that describes persons, places, and circumstances necessitates that we guard against possible misuse of information. Although the writer may be the only one to view the portraits, it's advisable to safeguard anonymity and confidentiality with fictitious names. The subjects of the Teacher Reflections study didn't object to my using their names, but I felt that to avoid possible unwanted repercussions, I should change them.

Before you construct a portrait to share, discuss your general intentions with the people involved. While different points of view exist as to whether it is necessary to share portraits first with those portrayed as long as permission to use data has been secured (Lightfoot 1983), usually the portrait and its audience seem better served by gaining others' reactions and suggestions before making the document public.

Sharing a portrait with the person(s) observed deserves careful consideration. If you have ever been embarrassed by an unflattering snapshot of yourself, you have an inkling of the problems that might occur when confronted with a written portrait. Portraits are the creation of the author, more akin to paintings than snapshots. No matter how objective we try to be in constructing them, we select from among details and bring our judgments and interpretations to bear on the subject. It isn't reasonable to expect that the results will always be appealing as well as accurate.

Written portraits, more so than painted ones, can be surprising because we often incorporate the person's own words. This was the case with the portraits in Part One, Section II. Rather than have the teachers read their portraits without the benefit of the context from which I had written them, I asked them to return to their journals, read them, and write their reactions. "How did you feel about what you wrote now that you have had the perspective of a year or two?" After the teachers shared their reactions with me, I gave each a portrait for their reactions. The reactions were interesting. I, as the portraitist, was nervous. What if they were disturbed by what I had written? What right did I have to probe into their lives? What parts of the portrait were my views and which were theirs? What had my eyes settled on, and were these images accurate? What would I feel if I were reading a portrait of me? Jerry's reactions were typical:

> Yes, that's me alright. I wish I hadn't said and done some of those things. But, I did. I found myself going back in my mind as I read it to the way I felt and to the children I had that year. Sometimes I long for that class again. So many special times. . . . I wasn't surprised by the portrait whereas I might have been if I had read it without first going back and reading my journal again. Some of that was painful, but this was not. I liked reading about me. I felt that I was another person—you know, reading about some-body else, yet it *was* me.

Plummer (1983) summarizes ethical considerations for persons using documents of life in response to the question "Is there a research mo-rality?":

- *Confidentiality.* (Is this always possible? In what ways can researchers protect confidentiality and retain the integrity of the work?)
- *Honesty.* (Is it always best to be as factually accurate as possible?)
- *Deception.* (One can be honest but also deceptive in what one does not disclose. Isn't much inquiry and research deceptive, and neces-sarily so? See also Peshkin 1983.)
- *Exploitation.* (To what extent is the subject of writing to benefit from the writing and research? Toward what ends does the inquiry lead, and for whom?)

Though writing about people for educational purposes is for understand-ing rather than for personal gain, it is important to keep ethical and professional concerns in mind. Most educators are aware of the effects that categorizing can have on a student's achievement and well-being; peg a student as a robin and she may never get to be a cardinal. A safeguard against this is to remember the significance of context and the dynamic nature of development—as these relate to both the observed and the observer. With these in mind, writing profiles, vignettes, and portraits can provide organized, empirical evidence for making profes-sional decisions.

If the subject of the portrait is a person (it usually is), we engage in what Jerome Bruner calls "life writing." And if the subject of the portrait is the author, we enter the realm of autobiography and life history. In the next chapter we will focus on ways to further investigate the personal dimension of professional development.

SECTION V

Personal and Professional Inquiry

It is teachers who, in the end, will change
the world of the school by understanding it.

Lawrence Stenhouse

The more teachers learn about teaching, the more articulate they become
about the why's of practice. This section is designed to assist journal
writers in becoming aware of their personal and educational histories
and the social contexts within which they teach; and to describe methods
of inquiry for understanding teaching and, when these methods are used
collaboratively, for shaping the profession.

received Pulitzer Prizes. Studies in adult development described in Vaillant's *Adaptation to Life* (1977) and Osherson's *Holding On or Letting Go: Men and Career Change at Midlife* (1980) present life histories of men, while Spencer's *Contemporary Women Teachers: Balancing School and Home* (1985) presents a rare look at the personal and professional lives of eight women teachers. *Teachers' Lives and Careers*, edited by Ball and Goodson (1985), provides insights into the life histories, careers, and identities of classroom teachers. Each of these works, especially the more recent studies that take us into schools, are valuable as catalysts to autobiographical thinking and writing.

AUTOBIOGRAPHICAL WRITING

In *Autobiography in Education* (1974), Peter Abbs writes of the nature of autobiography:

> The central concern of all autobiography is to describe, evoke and generally recreate the development of the author's experience. It is probably in all cases an attempt to answer the following conscious or half-conscious questions: Who am I? How have I become who I am? What may I become in the future? Autobiography is, thus, concerned with time: not the time of the clock, but the time in which we live our lives, with its three tenses of past, present and future. Autobiography, as an act of writing, perches in the present, gazing backwards into the past while poised ready for flight into the future. (6–7)

The word *autobiography* stems from *autos* (self), *bios* (life), and *graphia* (writing). "I am," whether written, drawn, or sculpted, is proof of life, of life's worth.

Until adulthood, we aren't able to view our own development as it occurs; we're too busy experiencing it. As adults, we can draw from memories, talk with others, search through old pictures and mementos, and visit the places where we grew up. Reading biographies like Russell Baker's *Growing Up* (1982), Eudora Welty's *One Writer's Beginnings* (1983), Janet Frame's *To the Is-Land* (1982), Miles Franklin's *Childhood at Brindebella* (1963), and Annie Dillard's *An American Childhood* (1987) enables us to recall images and experiences from our own pasts, to share common experiences. The following excerpts from Janet Frame's book on her New Zealand childhood and Russell Baker's on his northeastern United States childhood detail experiences that, in various versions, millions of us have lodged in our own memories.

From Frame's *To the Is-Land* (1982):

My memory is once again of the colors and spaces and natural features of the outside world . . . I discovered a place, my place. Exploring by myself, I found a secret place among old, fallen trees by a tiny creek, with a moss-covered log to sit on while the new-leaved branches of the silver birch tree formed a roof shutting out the sky except for the patterned holes of sunlight. The ground was covered with masses of old, used leaves, squelchy, slippery, wet. I sat on the log and looked around myself. I was overcome by a delicious feeling of discovery, of gratitude, of possession. I knew that this place was entirely mine; mine the moss, the creek, the log, the secrecy. It was a new kind of possession quite different from my beastie dress or from the new baby Isabel, over whom Myrtle and Bruddie and I argued so often (for Mother had said that Isabel was my baby, just as Bruddie was Myrtle's baby) that it seemed to me that owning people was too hard to manage if you had to keep fighting over possession.

[On an early family expedition to the south coast] I told my story of the bird and the hawk and the bogie . . . [I] remember the occasion chiefly because I remember seeing in my mind the huge, dark shadow of the bogie as it came from behind the hill: "Once upon a time there was a birdie. One day a hawk flew out of the sky and ate the birdie. (Oh poor little birdie.) The next day a bid bodie came out from behind the hill and ate up the hawk from eating up the little birdie."

I remember, too, the fierce attempt to make my audience, Myrtle and Bruddie, sit absolutely still and my asking Mother for help. "Mum, Myrtle and Bruddie's wiggling. Tell them to stop wiggling while I tell my 'tory." (25–27)

From Baker's *Growing Up* (1982):

It was a gentle Indian summer morning . . . I set off on one of my daily wandering expeditions, taking the road down toward the creek. . . . You could always find something entertaining to do. . . . Climb a fence. Take a stick and scratch pictures in the dirt. There were always cows around or a horse. Throw pebbles at a locust tree. I was busy at this sort of thing when I saw my cousins, Kenneth and Ruth. . . . When Kenneth walked right up to me, though, he stared at me with such a stare as I'd never seen.

"Your father's dead," he said.

It was like an accusation that my father had done something criminal, and I came to my father's defense.

"He is not," I said.

But of course they didn't know the situation. I started to explain. He was sick. In the hospital. My mother was bringing him home right now. . . .

"He's dead," Kenneth said.

His assurance slid an icicle into my heart.

"He is not either!" I shouted.

"He is too," Ruth Lee said. "They want you to come home right away."

I started running up the road screaming, "He is not! . . . He is not. . . ."

I was almost certain before I got there that he was.

And I was right. (59–60)

Writing autobiographically assists us in understanding the past and gaining greater appreciation of it, much as it enhances an awareness of the present. We begin to see patterns, connections. In the conclusion of an autobiographical work where the author sifts through her childhood and writes vignettes about her recollections of several significant people in her life, Kate Hulbert (1983) writes

The Legend of Brady's Landing

I know the truth. Not what really happened that day when Brady made his famous leap, but this: We all need, sometimes, to be in the middle of the stream breathing pure air. Auntie needed to sit in her familiar room and hold communion with her letter box. Brian needed to look at the world from his window. Maybelle needed to march in a flowing yellow dress and tell the truth at a town meeting. Grandpa needed to walk a single railroad track. Sandra Warren needed to sit in full moonlight and pluck the hair from her head. Mr. Willard needed an Ohio year of anonymity. And I, of course, need to write about it. (139)

Similarly, Ruth Kanin, author of *Write the Story of Your Life* (1981), found that as she compiled a personal history and family record for her family, the "project did more for me than a potpourri of therapies." She later studied autobiography and taught students to write their life stories. "Most students who undertook this project experienced relief from puzzles and ghosts haunting their past. Their goals were more sharply defined. When they were able to accept all of life's experiences, their rewards were major life changes" (xvii).

Changes in understanding and acceptance are particularly important to those of us in educational professions, whose responsibilities include purposeful reflection and intentional intervention in others' development and learning. Becoming aware of the factors (both internal and external) that influence us allows us a degree of control over them, hence ourselves. As we write, we discover that we are *all* of our experiences, impulses, and behaviors, just as are our students, friends, and colleagues.

Autobiographical writing can be in spontaneous response to an event, a moment in time (a student's remark that seems at odds with how we might have responded at that age, a news item that jogs memories), or a systematic attempt to reconstruct a period or periods of life.

Kanin suggests beginning an autobiography by dividing your life into eight categories and briefly filling in remembrances for each. This sets the stage for more in-depth writing on your life and for exploring "the sub-liminal self." The author addresses personal growth and self-esteem throughout the book. Whereas many of us approach autobiographical writing with trepidation at recording memories we would rather forget, this soon subsides as we write in response to exercises designed both to demystify writing and to integrate the ghosts in our closets.

Ira Progoff (1975) advocates another approach to "reconstructing a life." Rather than writing chronologically, the journal writer should explore the past, present, and future, and "inner" and "outer" experiences as in dialogue, moving back and forth in time and between conditions and events and the author's thoughts and feelings, which helps to establish the author in the ongoing flow of life. Whereas the result of Kanin's book is a polished, written story, an autobiography, the result of Progoff's book is a process by which "our life history continues to unfold":

> It [the journal] thus serves . . . as the laboratory in which we explore experimentally the possibilities of our life. It also serves as the sanctuary to which we go for our most intimate and private, our most profound and universal experiences. But most fundamentally, the *Intensive Journal* process is our inner workshop, the place where we do the creative shaping of the artwork of our life. (296–97)

SUGGESTIONS FOR JOURNAL WRITING

Most of the following suggestions for autobiographical writing have been developed through work with teachers, administrators, and teacher educators in journal writing.

Broad Views over Time

The following exercises encourage you to take a broad view:

- *What issues and challenges do you face* as an educator? What issues and challenges faced educators when you were at the level of the students you teach? If, for example, you teach primary school children, how do your challenges differ from those faced by teachers when you were in primary school? In what respects are they similar problems? Draw a time line and highlight relevant social and educational events. Address concepts like family, community, jobs and work, teacher, administrator, curriculum, subjects, processes and methods of teaching, and leisure.
- *The "Wheel of Life"* is an exercise suggested by Kanin (1981) to enable a writer "to get an initial, quick panoramic view" of the writer's life. It consists of dividing three concentric circles into eight parts (see Figure 10–1). In each of seven consecutive parts write aspects of seven equal segments of life lived so far. In the outermost ring place the years and your ages for that seventh of life. In the next ring closer to the center write a word or short phrase indicating the major event(s) that happened in your life during those years. Next, in the innermost ring, jot down the kind of period that each was (e.g., busy, traumatic, dull, intense). The eighth segment is for the future. With this as a base, you can begin to get a sense of the whole of your life cycle to date, and to identify turning points. As for thinking about the future, Kanin suggests that you make a chart for categories and accomplishments wished for "from now on." (For example, category: health; wished-for accomplishment: more energy, lose ten pounds.) An advantage of the circular form seems to be that it's easy to see the ups and downs, the cycles and recurring themes and to get a sense of the ongoing, evolving, and integrated nature of your life history. What thoughts come to mind as you review your writing? Do you notice any patterns or cycles in your past?
- Instead of, or in addition to, the wheel of life, *record the years of your life* from birth to the present. Beside each year record your age. Next, begin to group the years in what seem to you to be natural periods or phases (see Figure 10–2). Then, list each period and begin to fill in your recollections (see Figure 10–3). Work on all of the phases quickly; move back and forth as memories return. Finally, review your writing and briefly summarize each period. (If you write with a word processor it's easy to add ideas; have a separate page for each period, which you can then add to.) This accomplished, you should be able to identify a theme or a specific period to write further about (e.g., "new steps in my career," decision points, important people, important events, or adolescence).

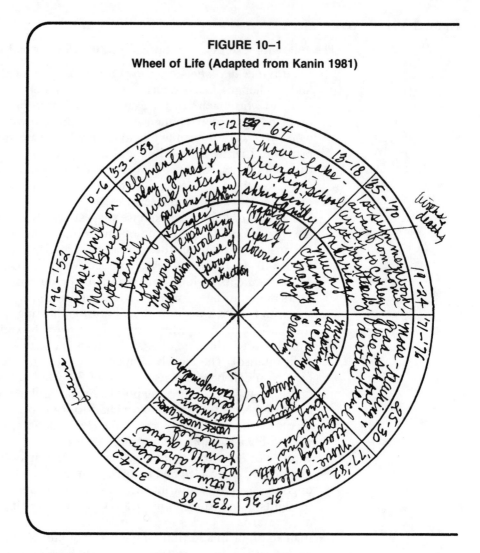

FIGURE 10–1

Wheel of Life (Adapted from Kanin 1981)

- *Select a period of your life* (e.g., childhood) and write about your most vivid memories. Record ideas and memories as quickly as they present themselves. Begin to group these (closest friends, family outings, school). This will generate other ideas. Write about your memories by group, or select one idea and write on it until you have either wound your way into other memories or you wish to write on another. At another time select another period (e.g., first job) and develop it in the same manner. After you write on two or three periods, provide transitions from one to another.
- *Flow charts and webbing* can be useful ways to generate ideas and

FIGURE 10–2

Autobiographical Log:
Life History—Year, Age, and Descriptive Category

Year	Age	Category	Year	Age	Category
1946	0	Early childhood	1969	23	Young adult, marriage, work
1947	1		1970	24	
1948	2		1971	25	
1949	3		1972	26	
1950	4				
1951	5		1973	27	Career branch, graduate
			1974	28	school, family move
1952	6	Elementary school	1975	29	
1953	7		1976	30	
1954	8		1977	31	
1955	9				
1956	10		1978	32	Job search, new position,
1957	11		1979	33	research, travel
1958	12		1980	34	
			1981	35	
1959	13	Family move, high school	1982	36	
1960	14				
1961	15		1983	37	Establish career, turmoil,
1962	16		1984	38	stability, change
1963	17		1985	39	
1964	18		1986	40	
1965	19	College			
1966	20				
1967	21				
1968	22				

memories for autobiographical writing. Select a topic and let ideas sprout from it (see Figure 10–4). In exploring professional development, for example, you might trace your previous work experiences, formal or informal education and schooling, people who have influenced you. After completing a chart, step back and review it. Do you see patterns? themes? cycles? Do some of the elements seem to fit together? In what ways? What thoughts and reactions do you have to what you see now? After drawing a few flow charts (or webs), do you detect connections, similarities? How, for example, might your schooling experiences relate to the jobs you have had and to influential people in your life? Select such a pattern and write about it.

FIGURE 10–3

Autobiographical Log (Excerpt):
Life Periods, Major Events, and Summaries

Age	Major Events	Summaries
0–5	Baby brother, big sister, extended family, deaths, being read to, swimming, the big snow	Family
6–12	Neighborhood play, cowboys, horses, reading and art, mom's college, sister's high school honors and job, lost baby teeth and Miss Berry, baseball, swimming, Sunday school and Sunday family dinners, raking leaves, weeding gardens and visiting neighbors, Mrs. Lyon's daughter, Coke and french fries, pop's fire, cheerleading, first loves	Expanding worlds, school
13–18	Womanhood, jr. high: new friends, hard math, tutored for diagramming sentences, IQ test trauma, family move and new school, new friends, learning to swim, choir, swim meets, love, Kennedy assassination, college prep, body and emotions and energy roller coasters, decisions and identity, shrinking family at home, mom teaches, sister's college and marriage, brother's move	High school, a potpourri of changes
19–22	Summer job away from home, break-up of love, away to college, deaths (first love, grandpa, grandma, roommate), summer schools, work at the dry cleaners, new roommates, football games, painting and drawing and literature and philosophy, failing "new" math, biology and geography, . . .	Transitions— growing, moving

FIGURE 10–4
Webbing Map of One's Life

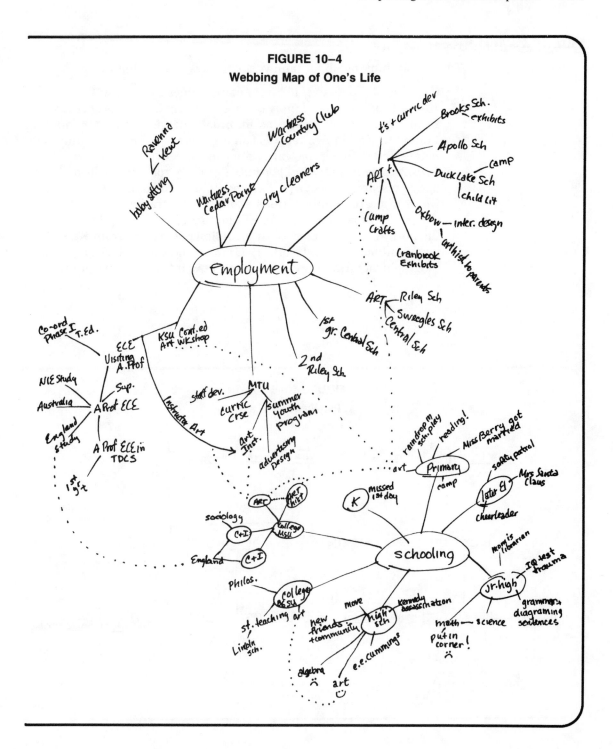

Family Experiences

To get you thinking about family experiences, try the following:

- *Construct a family tree.* Fill in as many names as you can (see Figure 10–5). Then ask other family members to help fill in gaps. Write their recollections about people as informal interviews in your journal. Community and town records can also be helpful in tracing missing names and defining unclear relationships.
- *Constructing biographical portraits* of family members can be fascinating research. Select a person who influenced your development, or whom you are simply curious about. Orchestrating the search and the portrayal is a creative process and results in a tangible product, the portrait (see chapter 9). In the following excerpt from Kate Hulbert's autobiographical work (1983) we see how autobiographical and biographical writing are related and how intriguing mysterious relatives can be.

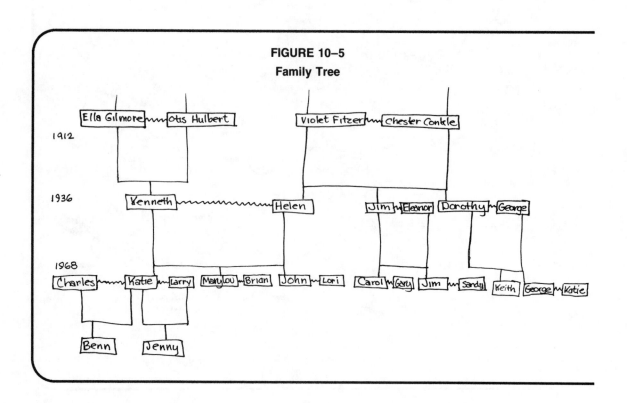

FIGURE 10–5
Family Tree

Joe

He became an obsession—this man who died thirty years before I was born. The hazy photograph that had been on Auntie's dresser disappeared with her papers and other photographs. . . . I would lie in the pineapple bed next to the window . . . and try to imagine what he had been like. Who was Auntie's Joe? I asked my mother and father and a few of Auntie's friends, but everyone said nearly the same thing—that they didn't know him very well. This of course could be a euphemism for nearly anything. When I asked what he looked like I was told that he had a nice face. . . . I began to realize that no one wanted to talk about Joe Morgan. And the more they wouldn't talk about him the more I wanted to know. . . . (40–41)

- Browse through old photograph albums and *select a picture for each period of your life*. Merge with the person you were at the time. What were the surroundings? What time of day was it? How do you know? What happened before the photograph was taken? After? Who else was important in the photograph? Describe everything you can remember about them, or at least what seemed most important to you then, and now. Explore in writing your thoughts as you remember the times—or as you imagine you remember. There is nothing wrong with inventing or embellishing. Indeed, it would probably be unnatural not to. Move on to another picture. After you have done this for several time periods, read them all in sequence of their occurrence and note your reactions. This can be as enthralling as it is enlightening, especially if you were able to talk with others who added information. What do others in the picture recall? What does the photographer remember?

- In reconstructing periods of your life, *identify critical events, turning points*, or as Progoff suggests, stepping-stones. What and who have been important influences on the person you are today? List both people and events. Write vignettes of those most interesting to you. Think chronologically, or note people and events impressionistically, outside of time.

- *Imagine yourself back* at the dinner table on a specific date in your early childhood. Draw a picture of the table and who was there. Include as much detail as you can remember. Describe the setting, people, food, conversation, including your own contributions, and your thoughts and feelings as you recall them. Try for sharp impressions, images, quotes, even if they're fragmentary. How does this dinner scene compare with a more recent one? In what ways are they similar? How are they different? In what ways have you changed? In

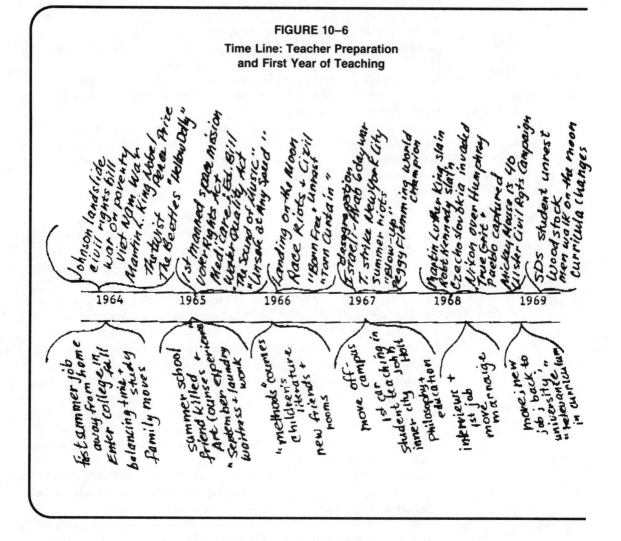

FIGURE 10–6

**Time Line: Teacher Preparation
and First Year of Teaching**

what ways stayed the same? What might you have talked about then
that you wouldn't talk about now and vice versa?

- How does your development parallel and interconnect with the ev-
olution of society? *Draw a time line* of your life or of a particular
period in it (see Figure 10–6). Mark off the periods and significant
events and experiences in your life below the time line. Above it briefly
note events and individuals in the nation and world at large that
helped to shape the world around you. In what ways do experiences
in your life reflect and relate to these? Another way to explore such

---

FIGURE 10–7

Excerpt from an Events Log

Years	Events in My Life	Events in Society
1968	1st teaching job marraige more curriculum development + teaching	1st state teachers' strike Martin L. King + Robt Kennedy assassinated Campus unrest + demonstrations John Holt _why Children Fail_ lectures

---

relationships is to draw up a table with three columns titled "Years," "Events in My Life," and "Events in Society" (see Figure 10–7).

Schooling and Educational Experiences

Here are some ways to begin thinking about your school experiences:

- *Bring out your school pictures*, records, and artifacts such as drawings, newspaper clippings, and report cards. Looking at a class picture, what do you remember about these people? Special friends? The teacher? The principal? School nurse? Custodian? What events took place that year? How would you describe the climate at school? You might wish to write about several years, or only one or two. How might your classmates have described you? How might your teacher have described you? You them?
- Looking at the same class picture, write about what it might have been like to be the teacher at this time. Has teaching changed? What would have presented challenges to this person? Have any roles and responsibilities changed? What do you notice about this teacher now that you didn't then? If you could converse with this person today, what might you talk about?
- Find a similar picture from your mother or father's school days. Ask them about this time in their lives. What differences and similarities are there between their recollections of school and yours?

- Allow about an hour for writing this exercise (or a couple of weeks —it's up to you). It consists of responding to three time periods: past, present, and future.

  1. The past. Write about yourself as an adolescent. Describe a few experiences and events, or people, that significantly influenced you as you evolved into adulthood (a geographical move, a family incident, a special relationship, a death).

  2. The present. Write about yourself as you are now. Describe your life. What major elements and contributing factors define you now? Describe yourself to a person who doesn't know you.

  3. The future. Write about the person you would like to be three years from now. How do you see your life evolving? As you read this writing, what are your reactions? Do any threads or patterns run through all three? Do you find any connections?

Professional Education Experiences

Also think about your professional life.

- What are the major issues and challenges you currently face as an educator? Describe them. In what ways do these influence your work? Do you find any connections between or among the issues you raised?

- What were *the most important issues, events, and circumstances in society during your professional preparation*? What were the reigning ideas and themes in education? the competing paradigms? In what ways might these have informed your education and shaped the teacher that you are today? Who were the most influential educators at the time and how might their work have affected you? How have they influenced your philosophy and approach to education? the aims that you hold for yourself and for those persons whose education you influence? In what ways have you yourself shaped your educational experiences?

- *Reflect in writing on your first year as a professional educator.* What did it feel like to begin a career? What hopes did you have? What were the challenges, large and small, that you faced? Who were the most important people in your early socialization and adaptation to the profession? Why were they important to you? What were your joys and frustrations as you became a staff member? What were the highlights of that first year? the low points? Consult old calendars, pictures, letters, lesson plan books, and other documents, including students' work. Talk with other people about their first years as professional educators. What commonalities and differences do you find?

What personal as well as professional adjustments did you have to make? A move? Marriage? New friends? What, if any, financial changes occurred? Adjustments to a different community? Or a different culture within the neighborhood and/or educational institution?

- *What have been the highlights of your career* since that first year? List each year and write a few comments to describe major events. Give particular attention to years where you had new responsibilities (e.g., became head of a curriculum committee, an officer in the teachers' association, or an assistant principal, supervised a student teacher, taught a college course, became a board of education member or politically active in the community or state). As you look back over your career in outline, what reactions do you have? Can you identify any themes or patterns in what you have written? Have any directions for the future become apparent to you? Who have been important colleagues? Why? In what ways have they contributed to your professional life? To whom have you been an important person? Why? In what ways have you contributed to their professional life? If you could list only a few, what would be the special events of your career so far? the most significant people?

- *Make a time line of your teaching career.* Start with your first year and stop at the present. What were the major incidents and changes that mark your career thus far? Divide the time line into parts. What distinguishes them? A change in responsibility? Growth in competence and confidence? New interests? What have been your major concerns over the years? Do you find different phases in your career and different types of concerns? Are they analogous to the theoretical conceptions of adult development or teacher career development such as Francis Fuller's (1969) scheme of changing teacher concerns (survival, teaching and curriculum, and concern for students' learning)? Erik Erikson's (1950) stages of psychosocial development? Jane Loevinger's (1976) categories of ego development? Talk with other educators and find out if they notice changes in their careers.

- The following *guided fantasy* is suggested by Newman, Burden, and Applegate (1980) as an aid for teachers to examine long-range development: close your eyes, and see yourself in your first year of teaching, on the first day of class. You're walking into the classroom. Look around; listen. Be aware of your feelings. Now see yourself one day near the end of your first year. What are you doing? What are you thinking? Now come to the present, and see yourself this morning at ten o'clock. Where are you? What claims your attention? Now jump to ten years from now. Are you still teaching? See yourself in your classroom.

Cultivating Different Perspectives

Try seeing yourself from different points of view:

- *Write a brief portrait of yourself* as a teacher. Include whatever you wish—philosophical statements, pictures, highlights of the year (or week), aims you have for next year (or week). Include a few excerpts or vignettes from your journal. Or select a vignette to work into a short story about teaching.
- *Construct a portrait of a teacher* you admire. Don't simply praise. Instead, provide specific illustrations of the teacher's practice, including examples of what makes this person admirable.
- *Write a paragraph or two about an important issue* facing educators. Now look at the same issue from other perspectives: the school board president, a teacher's aide, the superintendent of schools, a parent, a student, the principal, the custodian, the head of the state department of education, the teacher next door, the curriculum director, and the cook. In what ways might their views be influenced by their roles? After writing from three or four of these viewpoints, consider your point of view again. Have you adapted or changed it from your initial writing in any ways?
- In your mind *invite two friends from the past to dinner*. Select them because they will be interested in knowing that you are a teacher (or administrator or teacher-educator) and because you think that you will have an interesting conversation with them about all that has happened since you last saw them. Whom will you invite? Why? What will you tell them? What will you ask them? What will you serve?
- *Select a work of art* that exemplifies either what you would like your work (teaching, administration) to be, or what you think your work is. You can, for example, select a novel, a painting, a poem, a musical composition, a piece of sculpture, or an example of architecture. Write about the *objet d'art* and its relevance to your work.
- *Interview yourself on paper.* What do you most enjoy about your work? Think of times when you have felt especially good about your work and write about them. What do you least like about your work? Why? What are your favorite activities outside of work? those you dislike most?

Use your journal to explore, reconstruct, and extend experience. Record ideas, sayings, poems; use it to save cartoons and other artifacts you find meaningful or of interest. As many writers recommend, you might want to describe dreams in your journal. Keep a notepad on your nightstand so that you can record them before they fade. Progoff (1975) recommends a section of the journal for dreams and offers suggestions on how to document and learn from them. Taylor (1983) and Savary et al. (1984) write about dreams and their potential relation to personal growth. Pollard (1986) writes that "dream work" provides opportunities "to 'test out' our insights about the symbolic content of our journals in another context" (4). Using the journal to "probe the fearful and wonderful world within" can take many forms. Direct routes aren't always the best paths to understanding; divergent paths often offer more intriguing and fruitful journeys.

CHAPTER 11

Exploring the Profession

Sometimes one starts to dream about what culture, literary life, and teaching could be if all
those who participate, having for once rejected
idols, would give themselves up to the happiness of reflecting together.

Maurice Merleau-Ponty

The journal is a data base from which examples of professional practice
can be drawn and explored. Sections of the journal become evolving
portfolios for analysis and decision making. The journal enables the writer
to reflect consciously on aspects of work that were tacit, to capture reflection
in action. Barbara, for example, a first-year teacher, by rereading her
journal over a four-month period, found that clues relating to difficulties
she was having with a student came together. She saw problems develop
over time. "Now I see patterns in Tommy's behavior. I had no idea that
they started months ago. Now there's a baseline to work from." In this
chapter we will explore inquiry into the profession. Along with reflection
and introspection, collaborative action can enable educational change.

PROFESSIONAL CONTEXTS AND BASES FOR DECISION MAKING

There are several contexts for professional life and collegial involvement
(Figure 11–1). At the center lies the self. The first ring beyond that, the
family, like subsequent levels, is part of the person's professional world
and influences practice to varying degrees and in different ways. The next
two levels, school and district, provide several sources for professional
interaction, including staff and association meetings, in-service sessions,

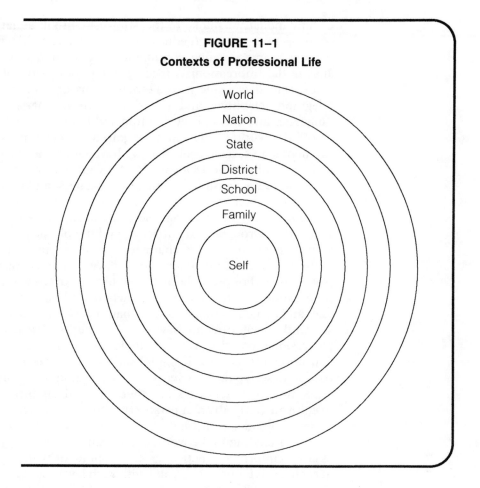

FIGURE 11–1
Contexts of Professional Life

consultancies, curriculum assignments and groups, and opportunities to engage in administrative deliberations and informal conversation.

The further we move toward the outer ring, the more removed might seem opportunities for professional engagement. Yet what happens in the outer rings influences what happens in the others. Teaching and learning are inextricably bound up in and influenced by natural and human-caused environmental matters—war and peace, poverty, technological advances, changing cultural values, for example. We come to understand the world through education. What were mysteries a few centuries ago are understandable today: lunar and solar eclipses, electricity, and flight, to name a few. We have a more comprehensive understanding of ecology—of how a change in one element has profound effects on others, of how industrial smoke in the Midwest can kill aquatic life thousands of miles away. Through education, language expands, the culture diversifies; we come to define, communicate about, and understand our world. Just as the Impressionists made possible new ways of seeing light and color, scientists made possible new forms of communication with the telegraph, telephone, and television. Each new perspective spawns new languages and ways of interpreting and living on earth.

As the world shrinks and we gain a greater understanding of environmental and social ecologies, we have more reasons to "think globally and act locally." The 1890s world of my grandmother's teachers differed from the 1920s world of my mother's teachers; and today's teacher faces different challenges from those my teachers faced in the 1950s.

The history of teaching, the cellular structure and organization of schools, classrooms, and curricula, and the physical, social, and psychological isolation that has characterized the profession (in teacher preparation and subsequent teaching) have mitigated against broadening perspectives. For example, an understanding of the ways in which teacher preparation programs socialize teachers and how state and federal policies and mandates influence and shape curricula and teaching—and consequently what students have an opportunity to learn—is necessary to professional practice. Yet these topics do not emerge as leading topics in educational discourse. If the focus is on survival or compliance, terms used to describe the first years of teaching and the requirements of mandates and competency testing, there is relatively little time or incentive to cultivate fairly abstract perspectives about how teaching and schooling relate to broader contexts.

Yet attending to the world outside one's community and state is necessary to informed practice. Professional identity incorporates affiliation at each level (Figure 11–2), and with each level come unique perspectives. Examine your own career. Being a child brought with it original perspectives on childhood. Being a college student brought new perspectives on education. Being a teacher brought still other views. Being a parent can provide different perspectives yet, as can being a supervisor or administrator. These multiple perspectives provide different lenses for interpreting and understanding life.

While attending graduate school as a classroom teacher I had the opportunity to study primary education in Great Britain. Although I had studied British education previously and done considerable reading before spending eight weeks there, I wasn't prepared for the changes in my perspective that would ensue. Having taught art throughout the elementary level, I was aware of developmental differences in children, but since entering the profession five years before, I had spent little time with children outside a structured school environment. In England I saw children

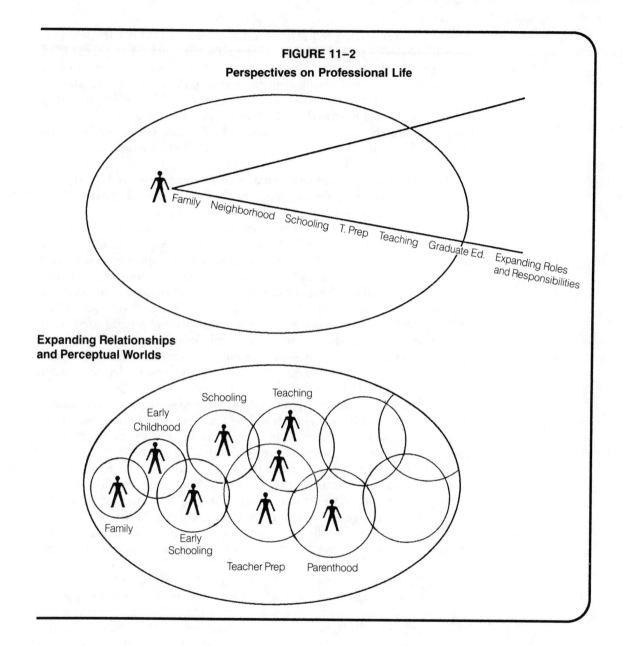

FIGURE 11–2

Perspectives on Professional Life

Family Neighborhood Schooling T. Prep Teaching Graduate Ed. Expanding Roles and Responsibilities

Expanding Relationships and Perceptual Worlds

Schooling

Teaching

Early Childhood

Family

Early Schooling

Teacher Prep

Parenthood

in less formally structured school settings. Not only did I learn about curriculum development but I also learned what children are capable of doing given encouragement and guidance. At the time, for example, it was surprising to find young children writing, *then reading*. This experience in another culture enabled me to view both children and teaching differently; when I returned to Michigan it was with new insights. I saw what had already been there but what I hadn't known to look for. The opportunity to talk with teachers who had different experiences and perspectives made this possible.

The importance of collegial relationships to professional, staff, curriculum, and program development is well documented (Lortie 1975; Holly 1977, 1983; Nias 1983, 1984; Little 1982). The question of conditions that support colleagueship has been raised by these researchers and others (Heath 1980; Eisner 1985). As John Gardner (1962) speculates: how can we fashion a system that provides for its own continuous renewal? For educators, personal growth and collegial relationships interact. Renewal necessitates breaking out of the social, psychological, and physical cells of much of institutional life; it means avoiding isolation and other obstacles to communication, while at the same time enhancing conditions for introspection. As they delve more deeply into their actions through reflective and autobiographical writing, educators can link with colleagues to explore phenomena from different perspectives and to define broader social contexts and planned change.

A colleague is an associate with whom we hold something in common. What we hold in common is enriched by the diversity of our experiences and views. Relationships with colleagues, whether with the teachers in one's building or across the ocean, expand what we hold in common, make possible new perspectives; they are catalysts for personal and professional growth, guards against isolation. They are essential to professional practice. It isn't surprising, therefore, to find that schools with norms of collegiality are noted for academic success (Little 1982). Collegial relationships are a first and necessary step to building and perpetuating "a system that provides for its own continuous renewal" (Gardner 1962, 7).

The "happiness of reflecting together" to which Merleau-Ponty alludes is more far-reaching than we might at first realize. Teachers are subject to the same developmental characteristics and needs as anyone else. Unlike many other adults, however, they spend most of their working hours with children. Lortie (1975) highlights several factors necessary to understanding the importance of collegiality: teachers are mainly women and in general suffer from low self-esteem; they are isolated, conservative, and present-oriented; they are not risk-takers or innovators. He also points out that their rewards are mainly psychic rather than monetary or material. Combs (1965), Jersild (1955), and Heath (1980) underscore the fundamental importance of psychological maturity and health to those who guide the mental and emotional development of the young, while Sprinthall and Sprinthall (1980) and Oja and Pine (1983) stress the significance of cognitive complexity to the functioning of teachers in dynamic relationships with others.

When we look at the history, sociology, and psychology of persons who teach and place them within the organizational structure of schools and the profession, we can begin to see how they interrelate. Take a person who, like most college students, has the normal complement of doubts about one's career, and put her or him into a workplace where full-time responsibilities are immediate—where there is the expectation, by both employer and employee, that the person is ready to teach. In these circumstances, to admit to difficulties is to compromise one's professional status; it is to risk one's already shaky self-esteem. To be present-oriented, conservative, conforming is simply adaptive behavior.

Is it surprising that teachers come to depend heavily on children in their classrooms for signs of their own personal and professional adequacy? Is it any wonder that new teachers are frequently criticized for wanting children to like them? Or that one of their resolutions for the second year is to be sterner with the children, to show them who's boss right from the beginning? Is it any wonder that the first year or two often sound more like warfare than helping relationships? To address teaching dichotomously (good–bad, stern–friendly, win–lose) because one must do so to survive is to foster (or perpetuate) a simplistic impression of what it means to teach.

When teachers are placed in a collegial environment, on the other hand, they immediately become privy to alternative perspectives; they can draw on the experiences and perceptual worlds of others; the multifaceted nature of teaching is opened to them. They can move comfortably beyond the first-year notion that "I should know how to teach. I have a degree now." These teachers don't have to rely solely on students to tell them they are doing well; they gain feelings of efficacy through their interactions with colleagues, through discussion and action related to teaching and learning, curriculum and staff development; through the feelings of strength that come from contributing to colleagues' practice and a professional ethos.

Using the journal to explore and organize professional life provides a base for collegial discussion, collaboration, problem solving, evaluation, and planning. The following methods of inquiry are offered as ways to develop different perspectives on practice and to overcome some of the constraints that have traditionally reinforced practice in isolation. The following assumes that when we focus on practice and reflect on it (1) new questions and insights occur, and (2) our inquiry naturally takes us into broader professional contexts and interactions.

METHODS OF INQUIRY

Classroom inquiry is as old as the classroom. Admittedly, there is more attention to formal research on the profession and to those who function within it than ever before, but teachers have always been seekers, questioners. Indeed, it is probably impossible to teach without inquiring. As Lucy Calkins (1986) writes:

> Teaching, like writing, is a process of rough drafts and revisions. Pulling in, pushing back; creating and criticizing, we ask the same questions of our teaching that we ask of our writing:
>
> - What have I said so far?
> - What am I trying to say?
> - How else could I approach this?
> - What am I learning? (141)

We discussed several ways to approach inquiry in the last three chapters: how to get started writing, methods of autobiography and life writing, and how vignettes and portraits can be useful in describing and analyzing schooling, teaching, and professional development. This chapter takes us further into what Stenhouse (1975) describes as systematic self-critical inquiry and collaborative methods for educational investigation. The teachers in chapters 3–5, Judy, Carole, and Jerry, were beginning to use their journals in more systematic attempts to understand practice: Judy in approaching case studies to study children, Carole in interviewing students, and Jerry by writing autobiographically and discussing teaching introspectively and analytically with colleagues.

The following methods for exploring professional life are suggested because they are open-ended, personal, collegial, and well suited to the dynamic and complex nature of teaching. "Inquiry in the Field" includes several ways educators study the profession. Different types of *interviewing* are described, followed by the *"I-Search,"* which is a way to tell a story about a professional inquiry—of the unfolding questions, procedures, and findings of such a search. The *case study* is a method used by social scientists and educators for gathering, organizing, and interpreting information relative to study of a person, group, event, or circumstance. *Action research* is a process for theorizing about and testing solutions to practical problems with the intent of improving educational conditions and learning from practice. *Clinical supervision* involves two or more persons in collaborative inquiry into practice.

INQUIRY IN THE FIELD

Field research is often referred to as *field work, qualitative method, interpretive research, case study method,* and *ethnography* (Burgess 1982). Like social anthropologists who blend in and study the customs of small social communities, we, as educational researchers, can study the field within which we practice—classroom, school, or college of education. Unlike researchers new to the settings they study, we face the challenge of generating new ways of investigating the familiar. We must do what Thomas Kuhn, author of *The Structure of Scientific Revolutions* (1962), urges us to do, to "change in the perception and evaluation of familiar data" (viii–ix). Not only must we immerse ourselves in the settings we study, we must observe our observing. As Gulick (1977) put it:

> Life in the field involves the same emotions as life at home: elation, boredom, embarrassment, contentment, anger, joy, anxiety and so on. To these are added, however, the necessity of being continually on the alert (of *not* taking one's surroundings and relationships for granted). . . . These necessities are likely to force a heightened awareness of facets of one's personality of which one had not been aware before. (90)

To understand and to interpret our observations of others, then, means that we must develop the capacity for self-awareness and self-criticism. We must involve ourselves in the setting *and* detach ourselves from it so that we may observe from outside the immediate circumstances. "Perhaps," writes Evans-Pritchard (1973), "it would be better to say that one lives in two different worlds of thought at the same time, in categories and concepts and values which often cannot be easily reconciled" (2–3). We are observers, participants, and, with others, the observed.

Interviewing

There are at least three different types of interviews that can be useful in educational research: structured, semi-structured, and open-ended.

Structured interviews are designed to focus the interviewee's responses on fixed questions. As researchers, we design questions ahead of time and ask them of everyone interviewed. Lortie (1975, 251–52) suggests questions like the following for a structured interview:

- Of the various things that you do as a teacher, which do you consider to be the most important?
- Every so often, teachers tell me, they have a really good day. Could you tell me what a good day is like for you? What happened?
- In one research project, it was found that teachers consider the principal an important factor in choosing between possible positions. What questions would you ask about the principal if you were considering working in a new school?
- What kind of knowledge do you think a teacher must possess—what does he or she have to know—to be able to do a good job?

Semi-structured interviews provide more latitude, allowing for in-depth probing of any matter that becomes relevant as the interview proceeds. Coles (1967) uses the following kinds of questions:

> What do teachers and school administrators . . . think about their students' abilities, their possibilities and faults and limitations? . . . What do they expect of those children, and what do they see their future to be? What hope is there for those boys and girls—and how much effort, care, and attention do they require? . . . What, if anything, works in the classroom with "low achievers" and "disruptive children," with the "disadvantaged" and the "deprived"? If something does work—some technique or philosophy or method or rule or plan—well, how does it work?
>
> And the children, what do they see happening around them, to one another and to their teachers and to the world? What does the future hold? Of what use is school, and why do children go to it, except because they must? What is interesting in school? . . . What are teachers like? . . . Is there any teacher you've ever had who somehow really turned you on? . . . How come? What was he or she like, and why aren't more teachers like him or her?
>
> These are some of the questions I had in mind as I went to schools . . . and talked to dozens of . . . children . . . teachers . . . and principals. (446–48)

An *open-ended interview* can proceed from specific or general ideas that we would like the interviewee to address. We might begin by recording topics to explore with the interviewee. The topic might be as general as the government's influence on educational programs or as specific as "the experiences you felt were most worthwhile in the in-service education session last Friday."

The manner in which questions are asked can influence how people respond. The interviewer shouldn't lead the respondent with phrases such as "I hate this new reading series. What do you think?" Consider timing and circumstances: the first week of classes, Friday afternoon, the night before vacation, or when grades are due—each brings with it an unspoken set of tensions. The close of a long and/or fraught staff meeting would probably be an inappropriate time to address colleagues with "Got a minute? I have a few questions."

I-Searches

As a professor of English, Ken Macrorie found it difficult to motivate new college students to write traditional research papers, for they seemed removed from real-life concerns. Research involved digging around the library stacks for information on subjects already countlessly researched and written up. As Macrorie (1984) puts it, such papers were typically "an exercise in badly done bibliography, often an introduction to the art of plagiarism, and a triumph of meaninglessness—for both writer and reader" (i). I-Search projects were designed to combat these difficulties and to encourage students to "examine and respect their experiences and needs" (ii).

I-Search is a form of inquiry based on a researcher's real concerns. It is, in other words, a true search, a seeking after answers that will matter to someone. The key to the I-Search project is that it begins with honesty and curiosity:

> No one can give other persons knowledge, make them think or become curious. Knowledge must reside in a person or it is not knowledge; and even if that person accumulates it, without use it is—what else could it be?—useless. . . . Until persons become curious, start thinking, do something with their knowledge, there is no such thing as curiosity, thinking, or use of knowledge. These activities don't exist in the abstract but in individuals, who then become alive. (Macrorie 1984, 14)

As you continue to write in your journal you will probably notice recurring themes that beg to be investigated. Take one of them and describe it. Why is it an interest? What do you know about it? What do you want to know? How might you go about gaining information? Whom might you involve? What processes will you use as you search? The last part of the project description is documentation of your sources.

Macrorie (1984, 64) divides writing into four parts:

1. What I knew (and didn't know about my topic when I started out).
2. Why I'm writing this paper. (Here's where a real need should show up; the writer demonstrates that the search may make a difference in his or her life.)
3. The search (story of the hunt).
4. What I learned (or didn't learn. A search that failed can be as exciting and valuable as one that succeeded).

After the I-Search is written, review it. Are there places where additional information would clarify the story? where editing might enhance the story's flow? When you are satisfied with the work, find a colleague to share it with, perhaps someone who was part of the search and for whom the story would be particularly significant. I-Searches can leave important impressions of your work that you will return to long after the issues have changed. They serve as chapters of your professional life and documentation of the questions that have concerned you over time.

Case Studies

During her five years of teaching in a nursery school classroom, Cindy has been concerned about the adaptation of many young children to social worlds outside their families.

> When I discovered that I was going to have Lea in my classroom I had many questions and concerns about her adjustment. Initially I wondered how she would cope with a very difficult situation. So many times I've asked myself how she has been able to adjust so well. I have often tried to put myself in Lea's place to imagine how she felt inside. I think that Lea was able to cope because she was given a great deal of support from her mother and me.

Though Cindy has studied children informally throughout her teaching career, Lea is her first written case study.

> Lea is a child who is now living thousands of miles from her native home. This is the first time that she has been away from her home and family. . . . Her family is one that is very close. Both sets of Lea's grandparents live close to her home [in Greece]. Lea is especially close to her maternal grandmother with whom she spends a great deal of time. Lea is the only grandchild. . . .
> Lea had an extremely difficult time adjusting to her new school environment. During her first few weeks she spent a great deal

of time crying. When she arrived in the mornings she had trouble separating from her mother. She would typically enter with her pacifier in her mouth, stand in front of her mother, stroke her and talk to her mother while crying. After Lea had a few minutes to say goodbye I would take her by the hand to the library area. . . . She often chose a book about colors for me to read. It was during one of these readings that she began to say the English names of the colors. . . .

During the first 2 months of the semester, Lea spoke a great deal of Greek to us. She would talk on and on about things which none of us understood. It was very fortunate for all of us that Lea understood a great deal of what we said to her. . . . There were times though that proved to be frustrating for Lea and us. . . . Lea was trying to ask or tell us things that would require an answer or help from us. When Lea realized that we just couldn't understand her, a look of helplessness would move across her face as tears welled up in her eyes. When all else failed I would take her hand and ask her to show me what she wanted. . . .

Lea's mother and I worked very closely together trying to help Lea adjust to her new life. Her mother became the interpreter for Lea and for me. . . . These shared messages along with our constant support finally seemed to make a difference. . . .

Lea began to separate from her mother much more easily. . . .

One day Lea's mother accidentally forgot the pacifier. Lea made it through the day without ever crying for it. . . .

. . . [S]he began to speak more English. When Lea would see another child do something that she thought was wrong or that she didn't like she would say "No ———," naming the child involved. . . .

Small incidents of peer interaction began to take place. One day while eating her lunch she and Mikey began swinging their legs under the table. They laughed and laughed with one another. . . .

One day, one of her classmates hurt himself. . . . Lea came over to him and began stroking his arm as she made a sad face. She then reached up and wiped the tears away from his face with her fingers. . . . She comforted him so beautifully without using any words. . . .

In mid-October, a mutually rewarding friendship seemed to have suddenly been born. Lea and . . . Ann discovered each other. . . . One morning after Lea had drawn a picture she held it up saying, "Look Ann, flowers." . . . Outside one day when Ann and Lea were playing together Ann looked at me and said, "I guess I won't have to learn to speak Greek cause Lea's learning English." . . .

As I reflect back it is hard to believe that Lea has made so many positive changes in only three months. . . . I watched her closely for signs that would indicate to me that she was ready to try something new. . . . Being with Lea has brought with it new challenges and experiences. Because of Lea's circumstances I have had a rare opportunity to learn more about myself and about her.

Cindy's case study began informally as she wrote in her journal about Lea and other children and her teaching experiences. Then she decided to look more closely at Lea, to describe her behavior and her own attempts to help the child. She decided to do a case study of Lea.

To begin, she wrote everything about Lea that she could think of: her first day of school, her mother's reaction to bringing her to school and to their conversations and actions as the days wore on and Lea continued to have problems in adjusting to school. What did Cindy know about Lea's family? How long had they been in this country? What had Lea's mother told her about Lea and the family? What behaviors could she remember? What seemed to affect Lea, even slightly? What subtle clues could she remember? Her writing described the context of the problem. She included her own thoughts and behavior. What were her reactions to Lea, what did she say and do? As she responded to these questions, she defined the case as clearly as she could.

Where would she go from here? She decided to document Lea's behavior more systematically. Each day for several weeks Cindy kept anecdotal records in her journal on what seemed to be relevant information. During this time she continued to note her own behavior and to provide support for Lea. Slowly, clues began to fit together.

Like Cindy's study, case studies are typically undertaken by educators in response to problems that necessitate focused study for understanding and require practical action. They are appropriately undertaken in response to inquiries that pose the questions "How?" and "Why?" Case studies are especially useful for unraveling complex, unstructured mysteries for which there is neither one right approach, nor one solution. The researcher acts as a detective who uses ingenuity and creativity in investigating, uncovering, and integrating clues, searching for discrepancies, and using professional skill and judgment in generating and testing alternative hypotheses.

While most educator-conducted case studies focus on individuals, they can also deal with couples, groups, institutions, even nations. The written work can range from several sentences to several hundred pages. They can be explanatory, descriptive, and/or exploratory. And they can be used as a teaching tool as well as a research tool. In fact, "the case study method has its origins in the methods used to teach Harvard lawyers" (Easton 1983, 2). According to Yin (1984), the case study method has application in all phases of research: problem definition, design, data collection, data analysis, and composition and reporting. Whether one approaches the case study method educationally (Smith 1984), sociologically (Burgess 1986), scientifically (Yin 1984), through business (Easton 1983), or psychosocially (Runyan 1982), there are several characteristics that make it a very useful tool for studying the complexity of human development and learning in educational settings.

Defining the Inquiry. Many researchers, like Cindy, initially write around the subject to clarify the focus. When we are not quite sure what to call into question, what the challenge is, freewriting can help us move past a vague sense of unease or puzzlement to the framing of tentative perspectives. In stating the focus and posing questions we provide the bases for the case study and chart its direction. Often, the focus of study changes as the case progresses. Indeed, we may end up confronting matters that we didn't know existed at the outset. For that matter, clarifying the focus is important even if we decide not to take the study any further than this. As we conceptualize the focus, we reject, accept, search for new data, and integrate information, and, not infrequently, find that the original problem is really part of something else.

Design. How will you proceed to study the case? to gather information? To whom will you go? What are the most important elements of the inquiry (as you tentatively defined it) and what are potential data sources? What about the context, the historical antecedents? What of possible future concerns? (For example, Cindy felt it important to know how long Lea's family was to stay in the United States.) Will you include yourself in the study? If so, how will you keep track of your thoughts and feelings as you proceed with the study? your behaviors and hunches? What of your writing is interpretation and what is fact? Should you separate these in your journal or only in a finished version?

Because of the open-ended nature of many case studies, the design might best evolve as you go along. Simply recording in your journal the broad areas, possible sources, and ways to gather information, and proceeding wherever it takes you might be the most useful modus operandi. Whatever the design, it (and you) should be flexible enough to change as the unfolding inquiry dictates. The challenge is to be open so as to seize clues as they appear, but to be focused enough to avoid being sidetracked by irrelevant information.

Data Collection. Data collection begins before the problem is defined and can continue throughout the study. Gathering and making sense of information in a case study is a dialectical process. Researchers often begin with a relatively open view, narrow their focus, then expand it again. In my work with beginning teachers, for example, I started with the broad question "What is it like to be a beginning teacher?" and then focused on specific happenings within individual teacher's classrooms: "What were Nan's reactions to Leo's behavior during science today?" From here I went to a broader question: "How do beginning teachers handle discipline problems?"

Exploring the territory in a case study necessitates becoming aware of the meanings and structures within another's perceptual world. As curious, caring strangers, we gather clues that we hope will enrich our perceptions of the shifting focus of our study. We question to understand. We suspend judgment and enter with an attitude of wonder, of skepticism. We triangulate, looking from different angles at the same phenomenon. How do other children interact with Lea? How does her mother interpret her behavior? What does Lea do that doesn't fit with my hunches about what might facilitate her adapting to a "foreign" classroom? What developmental challenges is she facing? (*Trust*—how might I contribute to it? *Autonomy*—how might I encourage it? How might use of symbolic forms such as language and the graphic arts, as typically explored by three- and four-year-olds, be helpful?) What are signs of development (less crying, more involved social interaction, increased animation in body language, speech)?

There are at least four sources of information for case studies: yourself, the person(s) you study, the context (materials, routines, literature pertaining to child development), and other persons (in Cindy's case this included Lea's mother, the nursery school director, the classroom teaching aide). Making regular journal entries, which include information from each of these sources, builds a substantial data base for your questioning, reflection, and interpretation. Include analytical notes and hunches so that you can identify patterns before they might eventually become obvious. As far as possible make a record of actual behavior and of the person's words as well as other relevant conversations.

Where there are conflicts or discrepancies in what appears to make sense, describe them. Look for patterns, themes, recurring and related phenomena. Interrogate yourself. "What do I see here? If this is so, how can that be?" Marshal all the evidence you can find to dispute your hunches. Also gather evidence from multiple sources to support your contentions. When you begin to see patterns, ask yourself, "If this is true, then what else might be related?" If, for example, you suspect that a child who is losing weight is being abused, what other signs support the suspicion?

We humans tend to see what we want or expect to see, which is why it is essential to maintain a skeptical attitude. Even at the conclusion of a case study, the researcher should reiterate that the case is described from a certain perspective, at a certain time, and under certain circumstances. Case studies, as detailed as they can be, are still highly selective pictures.

As with any document written about people, a case study must be approached, conducted, and written with utmost respect, sensitivity, and confidentiality. Whereas it can be an extremely useful research tool for gaining insights and understanding into others and ourselves, it can also be damaging when misused.

Action Research

A case study is often undertaken to learn more about a person or circumstance without any intention of changing either. Action research, on the other hand, is conducted with the purpose of improving the quality of life within a social setting. Change is built into the process consciously. Case studies are often undertaken in action research, and when they are, the ultimate goal is improvement—transforming a situation from what it is to something the practitioner prefers (Schön 1983).

According to Dave Ebbutt (1985), pioneering efforts in action research can be traced to two somewhat independent sources. The first, a man named Collier, was Commissioner of Indian Affairs from 1933 to 1945. Collier represented a group that was emphasizing the importance of social planning, and he insisted that "research and then more research is essential to the program. . ." (quoted in Ebbutt 1985, 154). He used the expression *action research* and was convinced that "since the findings of research must be carried into effect by the administrator and the layman and must be criticized by them through their experience, the administrator and the layman must themselves participate creatively in the research impelled as it is from their own area of need" (Ebbutt 1985, 154).

The second source, the social psychologist Kurt Lewin, "was concerned with practical situations of social conflict," and particularly

> "in the psychological problems confronting any minority group whose space of free movement is restricted by barriers of caste and prejudice" (Lewin 1948, Foreword). Much of his work was carried out with Jewish or black minorities. The action component of his work derived from his insistence on democratically guided social change and his belief that "remedial efforts should be introduced into a community prepared to study the results of its own social action" . . . he developed change experiments de-

signed to allow groups from the communities in question, with the guidance of external consultants, to "learn to become detached and objective in examining the foundations of their own biases." (Ebbutt 1985, 154)

During this same time period, according to Ebbutt (1985), people in psychoanalytically oriented helping professions (i.e., psychiatry and clinical psychology) were developing ways to help individuals communicate more adequately. People were assisted in discovering gaps and discrepancies between their perceptions and actions and in their relationships with others: in uncovering personal and interpersonal communication problems that maintained biases and distortions in perception (Lippit 1949).

Educational action research builds on and includes elements of both individual and group self-study and social action. The gap between theory and theory in action (practice) is the rationale for using action research in classrooms and schools (Ebbutt 1985). According to Kemmis, "Put simply action research is the way groups of people can organize the conditions under which they can learn from their own experience" (Kemmis et al. 1981, 2). More recently, Kemmis (1985) writes:

> Action research is a form of self-reflective enquiry undertaken by participants in social (including educational) situations in order to improve the rationality and justice of (a) their own social or educational practices, and (b) their understanding of these practices, and (c) the situations in which the practices are carried out. It is most rationally empowering when undertaken by participants collaboratively, though it is often undertaken by individuals, and sometimes in cooperation with "outsiders." In education, action research has been employed in school-based curriculum development, professional development, school improvement programs, and systems planning and policy development . . . as a way of participating in decision making about development. (35–36)

Synthesizing writing on action research, Ebbutt (1985) defines it as "the systematic study of attempts to change and improve educational practice by groups of participants by means of their own practical actions and by means of their own reflection upon the effects of those actions" (156). Action research is different from many other types of research in this joint practical and theoretical orientation, in its direct and dialectical relationship of theory and practice, and in its contribution to social science.

The Ford Teaching Project (1971–75) was an action-research project designed to "contribute to the development of a theory of inquiry/discovery teaching and provide support for teachers trying to realize the aims of this kind of teaching in their particular situations" (Elliott & Adelman 1973, 8). As university members of the project team, Elliott and Adelman set out to foster in teachers the development of greater autonomy and control over their work in classrooms through reflecting on the consequences, intended and unintended, of their actions. Working with a group of forty teachers they defined their action-research tasks into three areas:

1. What are the problems that teachers encounter when they try to employ inquiry/discovery methods? Can these be generalized across subject areas, age levels, etc.?
2. What are effective strategies for resolving these problems, and to what extent can they be generalized?
3. What are the aims, values, and principles of inquiry/discovery teaching in general? (Elliott & Adelman 1973, 8)

Teacher participants volunteered for the project because they were interested, and in fact using, the inquiry/discovery approach in their teaching. As the project developed, many of the participants became aware of the difficulties in practicing what they said they believed; they found discrepancies between their theoretical notions and their behavior in classrooms. By the end of the project, most teachers had become "increasingly self-monitoring, able to test general hypotheses and identify new problems and principles" (Elliott & Adelman 1973, 12).

The project used triangulation to obtain the views of persons from different perspectives. How, for example, does the teacher describe a specific history lesson? How does an outside observer (either another teacher or administrator or university team member) describe the same lesson? How does a student describe the lesson? On what points is there corroboration of responses? Each is in a position to contribute unique perspectives. This combination of viewpoints provides a more comprehensive picture of the history lesson.

The university researchers monitored the process and described four problems they encountered in helping teachers "seriously reflect on their own classroom practice":

1. Teachers find it difficult to create the openness and honesty necessary for accurate feedback about their performance from pupils.
2. Self-monitoring threatens a teacher's self-esteem and feelings of professional confidence. As one of the project's teachers wrote: "Nothing is ever in a state of stasis, nothing is ever finalized, always there

is reappraisal in the light of new experience. Like children, we hanker after a finiteness of things."

3. The institutional context in which many teachers operate is not conducive to increased awareness of both self and situation.

4. Teachers find it difficult to make their classroom problems and experience accessible to one another. (Elliott & Adelman 1973, 25–28)

They found that serious reflection takes support, trust in both the environment and the person, as well as self-esteem, confidence, and time.

Addressing method, Kemmis (1985) writes that a self-reflective spiral of cycles of planning, acting, observing, and reflecting is central to the action-research approach. Lewin described the process as planning, fact-finding, and execution. Building on Lewin's ideas and describing action research as a framework for self-evaluation in schools, Elliott presents a heuristic model for viewing the cyclical processes involved (Figure 11–3).

Elliott's model incorporates his concerns that: (1) the general idea should be allowed to shift, (2) analysis and fact-finding should recur throughout the spiral of activities rather than only at the beginning, and (3) implementation of action is not always easy, and one should monitor the extent to which the action has been implemented before evaluating it (Elliott 1981). Depending on the subject of research, the cycles might continue as the topic branches into different subjects, or a few cycles might suffice to make the changes necessary to improve the quality of circumstances that initially led to the research. There might be any number of action steps depending on the subject and progress. These will change from cycle to cycle according to a continuing redefinition of the topic under investigation. The types and methods of study are as diverse as the questions posed. Often the case study method is used.

Current action research takes at least three forms: teachers cooperating with researchers (researchers define the subjects or topics of research), teachers in collaboration with researchers (teachers and researchers work in mutually beneficial relationships where topics are jointly defined and analyzed), and teachers as researchers (teachers define and conduct their own research). A group of beginning teachers and I have been conducting case studies in our respective classrooms with the intention of improving our practice. In some cases individual students are studied, and daily logs and anecdotal records are kept: "Leo is disruptive, won't finish assignments, and bursts into tears at the slightest provocation. Why? What can I do?" In other cases, the teacher focuses on an aspect of teaching that is posing difficulties: "There are times during the day that I just can't seem to get the students working. I think it has something to do with transitions, both from one subject to another and after breaks like the beginning of school, recess, lunch, and special subjects like gym and art when they leave the room. Help!"

FIGURE 11–3
Action Research Cycle (from Elliott 1981)

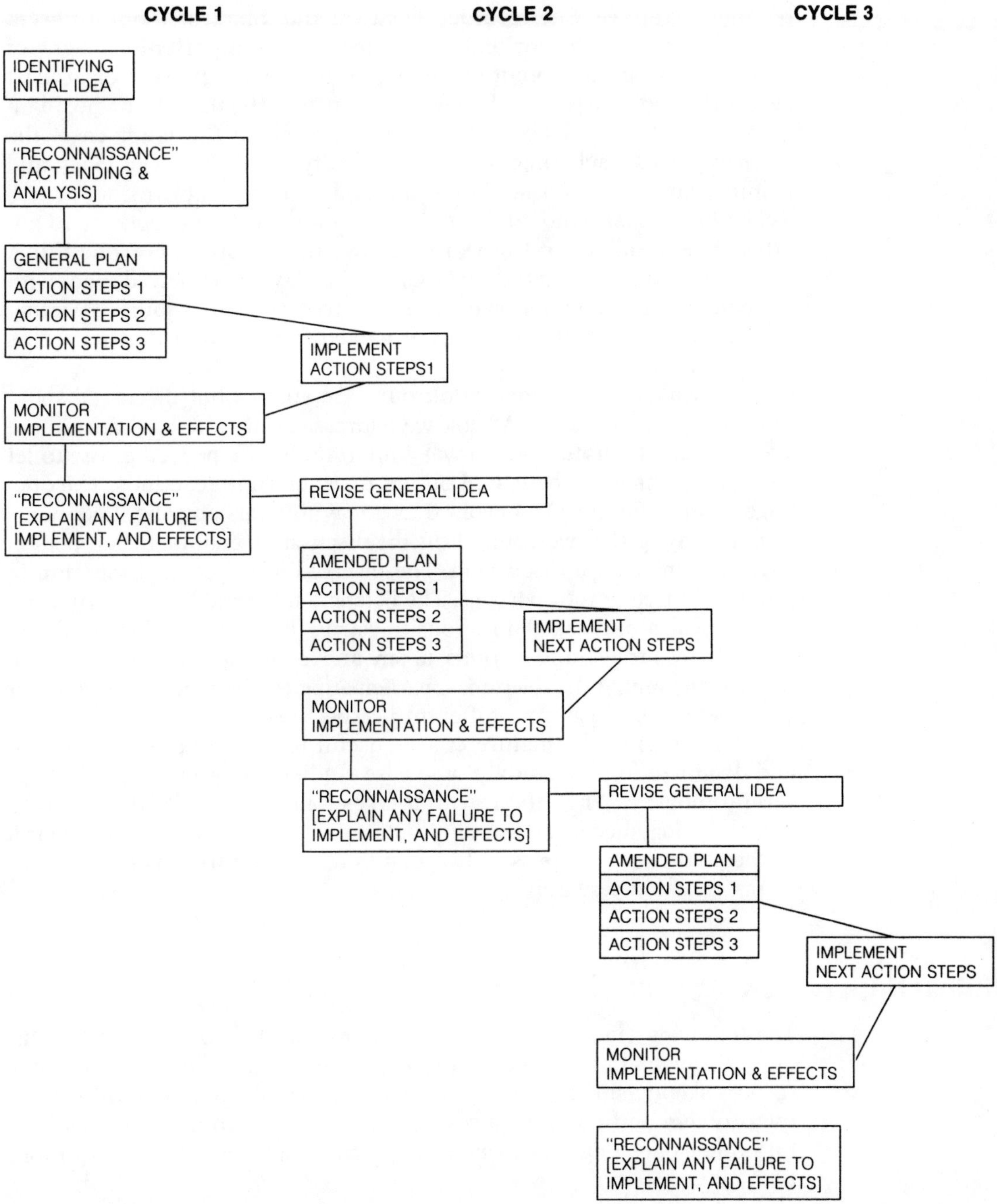

CYCLE 1   CYCLE 2   CYCLE 3

IDENTIFYING INITIAL IDEA

"RECONNAISSANCE" [FACT FINDING & ANALYSIS]

GENERAL PLAN
ACTION STEPS 1
ACTION STEPS 2
ACTION STEPS 3

IMPLEMENT ACTION STEPS1

MONITOR IMPLEMENTATION & EFFECTS

"RECONNAISSANCE" [EXPLAIN ANY FAILURE TO IMPLEMENT, AND EFFECTS]

REVISE GENERAL IDEA

AMENDED PLAN
ACTION STEPS 1
ACTION STEPS 2
ACTION STEPS 3

IMPLEMENT NEXT ACTION STEPS

MONITOR IMPLEMENTATION & EFFECTS

"RECONNAISSANCE" [EXPLAIN ANY FAILURE TO IMPLEMENT, AND EFFECTS]

REVISE GENERAL IDEA

AMENDED PLAN
ACTION STEPS 1
ACTION STEPS 2
ACTION STEPS 3

IMPLEMENT NEXT ACTION STEPS

MONITOR IMPLEMENTATION & EFFECTS

"RECONNAISSANCE" [EXPLAIN ANY FAILURE TO IMPLEMENT, AND EFFECTS]

In the first example, the teacher began to document exactly when Leo became disruptive. She recorded what she did. She tested out different responses to his behavior and even learned to read portentous signs of difficulties. From this point on she was often able to prevent or at least curb the child's disruptive behavior by shifting the activity or posing a question that guided Leo in another direction. In the latter case, the teacher logged each time she had difficulty controlling the class and guiding them into their studies and found that the problems happened, as she had initially thought, during transitions from one activity to another. She found several ways to improve the situation. For one thing, she scheduled events on the chalkboard each day and reviewed them with the children. For another, she planned activities such as journal writing and drawing to which the children looked forward and that served as transition times.

We worked independently on our case studies but discussed them during seminar sessions. At first we addressed only a few because there was so much to discuss. Each was important, so we needed a way to let each person have the benefit of others' questions and reactions. The one-page form in Figure 11–4 evolved as a way to focus on salient elements of the study so that we could limit the discussion, enabling each person to have a chance for discussion. These served to structure discussion in groups of three or four persons. The listeners mirrored back information to the speaker and asked questions to clarify the challenge (or problem), context, resources, and actions taken and contemplated. Rather than provide answers to the dilemmas, participating teachers helped each other to reflect on the case from different perspectives.

Log sheets of this nature can be useful in delimiting the challenge and documenting the study. Some case studies are brief; others last for several months. When the research takes longer than a week or two to complete, log sheets can simplify data analysis by providing a skeleton of the study as it progresses. It becomes a resource to consult for other forms of action research.

Clinical Supervision

The following vignettes describe problems that led to collaborative inquiry through clinical supervision. As in the I-Search, the journal writer records skepticism about the process as well as information to introduce the problem and circumstances and to trace how some questions lead into other ones (e.g., how one aspect of teaching might relate to more than one concern).

FIGURE 11–4

Case Studies and Action Research

Date:

Challenge:

Background and contextual information:

Resources:

Actions taken and consequences:

Possibilities:

Thumbing through her journal, Jessica, a middle school English teacher, noticed that Allan's name kept popping up. It wasn't that Allan was a poor student or that he was really a "misbehaver," but he never appeared to contribute anything to class, and he was always asking "irrelevant" questions. She got that "oh, no" feeling when she saw him walk into the room, though she had never admitted this, even to herself, until now. Where were his questions coming from? Why did they irritate her? Might she be doing something to contribute, inadvertently, to the situation? Perhaps Emily, her closest colleague, wouldn't mind making a few observations in this literature class.

David, a professor of curriculum, was committed to inquiry-based learning and proposed to offer a seminar in curriculum theory for advanced students who he assumed would be interested in delving into recognized theory as well as theorizing about their own practice. How might he structure the seminar for study and discussion? First he would assemble readings on major areas for study. Then he would arrange the schedule so that there would be plenty of time for participants to discuss their own research. He and students together would decide how to proceed with the readings and which, if any, they would discuss. David intended to provide an ideal balance of structure and openness for the seminar to work. As it evolved, however, discussion came to be dominated by a few students. Increasingly, he was thwarted in his attempts to guide, summarize, and wrap up the sessions on time. His suggestions were often spurned. Whenever he mentioned discussing their own research, students resisted. After class he took his frustrations out in writing and then used his journal to analyze the session. He was ready to (1) become an art historian, or (2) trade in the seminar for a lecture. What might Louise, a former colleague, think about these problems?

Sarah reflected as she wrote her reactions to an article on sex discrimination in the schools. She believed in individualized instruction and had designed and used learning centers in several areas of the curriculum. She felt confident in her teaching. Why was she even reading this article? And why was she feeling somewhat defensive at the thought of sexually discriminatory teaching? She had begun writing an angry refutation of the article. The more she wrote, however, the more her anger softened. "Well, yes, if children were being treated unfairly, it certainly is good that someone is doing research on it. . . . Come to think of it, I remember something of it from my own schooling. I wonder if I am contributing to that same kind of thing? How can I tell if I do treat the children differently?"

For years Howard, a school principal, had loved teaching. Then, one year he fell victim to a type of impotence endemic to our profession, based on the requirement that we give over this year's students to next year's inferior teacher. He struggled on paper with his frustrations: "So much of what I try to do falls apart! She [the teacher] spoon-feeds them! She doesn't allow them to think for themselves! She keeps them all at the same level. Lori leaves reading at an eighth-grade level and she's forced into a sixth-grade text!" Et cetera. That year was agony enough for Howard to enter into administration. If he were to really make an enduring difference in the lives of children, he would have to be in a leadership position. As a principal he'd have time to work with teachers; to find out what makes them tick and support their professional development. He'd connect Jean (Lori's teacher) with some in-service education opportunities that would help her to see the need for change. Yes, as a principal, there were many constructive things that he could do. But there were just as many things that he could not. His faculty meetings were just that—his. How could he foster teacher participation? Enliven the discussion? Why were they always looking at the clock?

According to John Smyth (1984), clinical supervision is collaborative learning about teaching. It includes what Elliott (1976) describes as "practical reflection." Whereas traditional forms of supervision are based on an outside supervisor observing and making comments and recommendations to teachers related to their practice, clinical supervision depends on collaboration. Sergiovanni (1982) describes it broadly as a way of life, a cultural structure and process for working with teachers and assisting them in evaluating their teaching and classroom life. Marks, Stoops, and King-Stoops (1978) explain it as trying to improve instruction through action and experimentation. Clinical supervision is formative of self-evaluation that relies on both oneself and the professional skills, attitudes, and knowledge of a colleague. The aim is to help teachers exercise power over their own professional development as well as their teaching (Smyth 1983) while at the same time removing isolation and developing communication among and between educators.

> The most distinctive feature of clinical supervision, both as a construct and as a process, is the way in which it invests in teachers the capacity to draw attention to those aspects of their teaching over which they can begin to exercise greater personal control. The implicit rationale of clinical supervision is that teaching processes can be improved when the teacher is provided with timely and relevant feedback on aspects of teaching that are of interest and concern to that teacher. (Smyth 1984, 5)

Clinical supervision includes four basic steps: the pre-observation conference, observation and teaching, descriptive analysis of teaching, and a post-observation conference.

Pre-Observation Conference. The pre-observation conference is key to successful collaboration. Mutual trust, reciprocity, and respect are essential. The aim of the pre-observation conference is to enable the teacher to talk with a sympathetic colleague who listens as the teacher thinks out loud (Smyth 1984). From this conference the teacher and colleague are to establish a clear idea of what they will explore collaboratively. In the case of Jessica, the middle school English teacher, she and her colleague Emily agreed to focus on Jessica's teaching of a lesson and in particular on how she questioned and drew the students into discussion. Emily needed to know several things about the lesson, the situation as Jessica described it, both in what she hoped would happen (her aims) and how she would go about trying to make it happen (her procedures and resources). They agreed that Emily would start by keeping a running record of the questions and responses that occurred during the lesson.

Observation. Because the students in Jessica's room were well acquainted with Emily, there was no problem with her sitting in the corner of the room taking notes on questions and responses. She also sketched the geographic space covered, mainly by Jessica, during the lesson. Sarah, the fourth-grade teacher concerned about possible sex discrimination in her teaching, selected Geraldine, a county curriculum consultant, to help her. Geraldine had been in the classroom on several occasions and had even worked with the children individually a few times. Her task, as they defined it, was to observe for an entire morning, ensuring that she would see informal and formal interactions, and therefore have ample opportunity to note any hidden or unconsciously sexist ways of relating in the classroom. She observed verbal interaction, body language, assignments, and transition times. On another day, she would observe for the afternoon.

Descriptive Analysis of Teaching. How to make sense of the data collected during the observation is another factor in the success of clinical supervision. Both the teacher and the observer must try to make sense of the data. Rather than being told what happened, the teacher sifts through the clues and comes up with her or his own webbing of ideas and reactions. The observer does the same. Together, they provide different perspectives on the same lesson. In reconstructing the lesson, each person is one step removed from it. By discussing the information and sharing perspectives they are able to gain still further distance from the events while probing more deeply into them. Howard, for example, asked Monique, the school secretary, to attend a faculty meeting to take notes on the discussion. She was able to record most verbal interaction in shorthand. Who initiated what discussion? Who asked what questions? After the meeting, she typed her notes and gave them to Howard. He analyzed these along with the agenda and his own written notes during the meeting (which he copied and gave to Monique for her analysis).

Before Howard looked at her notes, he reconstructed from his own the flow of events, writing briefly about his thoughts and feelings during the meeting. Then, he posed questions: "What happened? What did I set out to do? Did the meeting go as I expected? In what ways? In what ways didn't it? Would I do things differently? What might I have done differently? Why? Who participated and how? What signs of interest and involvement were there? Had I been the observer, what might I have seen? How might I interpret it?" Now he was ready to look at the data Monique had collected. This time-out for reflective, descriptive, analytical, and evaluative writing is valuable by itself, and, when combined with the perspective of another observer, it can be a powerful process for gaining insights and building a collegial environment.

Post-Observation Conference. After analysis comes the post-observation conference—a forum for sharing perceptions. It can include reconstructing the lesson (or circumstance), sharing themes and interpretations, and committing oneself to continuation or change (Smyth 1984). According to Grumet (1979), the purpose of clinical supervision is not to establish a collegial relationship, though that can be a consequence, but to help the teacher become a more critical observer of practice, to assume a dialectical relationship to that practice. The attitude and process of inquiry are more important than the questions raised.

SUMMARY THOUGHTS ON JOURNAL WRITING AND INQUIRY

In this chapter we discussed several ways to explore practice: interviews, I-Searches, case studies, action research, and work with colleagues in clinical supervision. By documenting and organizing inquiry in the journal we have professional bases for discussion, inquiry, and action. When we focus on individual students, as Cindy did in her case study of Lea, and when we work collaboratively with colleagues to describe and improve the quality of curriculum and teaching within the school, as did teachers in the Ford Teaching Project, the journal is an incomparable tool for documenting, organizing, and analyzing practice and the contexts within which intentional teaching and learning take place. The multiple perspectives that the journal enables the writer to explore, both in terms of time (past, present, and future), and points of view (situational, personal, and role-related), make new images of practice—professional practice—possible.

CHAPTER 12

Learning from Writing

> Oh yes, I've enjoyed reading the past years diary,
> & shall keep it up. I'm amused to find how its
> grown a person, with almost a face of its own.
>
> *Virginia Woolf*

Returning to read one's journal is an adventure. "[I]n diaries, as in life, people are much more changeable than they are in novels" (Mallon 1984, 30). Whereas novels and films are created and edited for public presentation, most journals are uncut. They are working documents. The freshness that results can be both invigorating and intimidating. After all, so much of communication is softened, mediated, and even distorted to make it acceptable, and journal writing, as we have described it, becomes authentic conversation with oneself. To read this conversation from a different perspective (as we do each time we return to it) is to expose ourselves to the scrutiny of a critical observer who has the benefit of distance and hindsight. Rereading a journal is like beholding a movie. When you write, it is from the actor's perspective on stage. When you reread, you are the audience: you have the benefit of moving through time, seeing the story develop over time without being caught in the action. In a sense, you are reliving the action, but with an outside observer's perspective.

When asked to reread his project journal well after it was completed and write his reactions to what he read, Craig did so with alacrity, curiosity, and openness.

> After reading my entire journal [about 340 pages] last night, I have a few distinct impressions. First of all, so much has happened in the four years since it was written. It was revealing and interesting to relive some of the experiences that pushed me along

toward where I am today. I fear that I am too anxious to get places and too forgetful of the importance of the past. Secondly, and along the same lines, much of the writing is trivial, thoughtless and immature. Most disturbing is how polemical I was at times, not in anger, but in a know-it-all sense. I feel as though I have grown up a great deal since then. . . . Thirdly, I simply ignored the question "How did you feel?" . . . I still have a great deal of difficulty with "how do you feel?" and find the question very threatening, but I am doing ever so much better with it than four years ago. Fourthly, the quality of the writing improved dramatically over the course of the journal entries. I guess practice makes progress. Fifthly, many of the thoughts . . . are exquisitely insightful and enduring in their validity. Finally, I stopped writing rather abruptly; the reason is part of all that has happened since then. . . .

I continued to read with a strange fascination and almost detached feeling, thinking how frustrated and unhappy I must have felt, and how I tried, nearly successfully, to hide those feelings. I was particularly impressed, and more than a little ashamed, at how bitter I was at the start of the 82–83 school year. That also was the year that I did something about my problems with teaching.

Since Craig wrote this, another chapter in his story has evolved. He is now an elementary school principal and writing again. He documents his work in administrative meetings and writes portraits of people involved in making policy, curriculum, and staff decisions. He continues to learn through his writing.

Learning is more likely when the writer listens with a quiet heart (nonjudgmentally). While you probably won't wait four years to reread all of your journal, there are benefits to returning to it with the distance that only six months, a year, or more can provide. Come back to your writing whenever the interest occurs. Read the journal as you might a story or life portrait of an interesting stranger, as if you didn't know its content or conclusions. Allow yourself surprise at change, at concerns and questions that have bloomed over time. Look, like Craig, for signs of growth.

CONFIDENTIALITY

Unlike Tolstoy, who kept two diaries, one for external happenings and one for their interpretation, most journal writers include the two together. This can lead to problems. If the journal is both personal and professional, confidentiality is a fundamental consideration. Discover ways to be private without the inhibitions and distortions that will hamper your writing. You must be free to explore and hence you must also feel comfortable about your explorations being safe from uninvited viewings. Invent ways to be private. Many journal writers use fictitious names or initials and fabricate extraneous, intentionally misleading details. Others find a safe place to store their writing. Though a journal can, as one first-year teacher recently put it, "be a much better place to put my anger than on that mother!" in the wrong hands it can cause devastating hurt and embarrassment. Except rarely, journals are not intended for public audiences.

LEARNING FROM THE JOURNAL

When you return to read your writing, record your reactions and additional thoughts. Some teachers do so in another color in the margins. Date your comments so that later you can see the writing from different vantage points. It is like having a conversation with two or three people at once! And, in fact, it is. What themes run through your writing? What questions and concerns? May Sarton (1973) notes the value of exploring the themes in her journal:

> A little warmer this morning. . . . I slept and woke and thought about this journal. There are obviously certain themes that recur and must be continuously explored. Around them, over the years, I have accumulated the wisdom of other minds . . . it may be appropriate now and then to draw on this store. (88)

What are your initial reactions to what you have written? Record these and then pose questions to guide your thinking:

- What do you write about? Do these topics (or concerns) change over time?
- Do you find philosophical writing at times and practical writing at others? Are there any patterns or cycles associated with these?
- Where and when in your journal do you record thoughts and feelings about teaching, and where and when do you write descriptively about students? Which ones?
- Whom do you write about? Why? In what ways do they influence your work and you, theirs?
- What types of writing (descriptive, evaluative, analytical, therapeutic, creative, introspective) can you identify?
- In what ways can you describe the images, tones, and styles of writing? When is the content of your writing firm? tentative? questioning?

- What can you learn from the handwriting? Is the writing small, large, tight, loose, open, planned, tentative? When is there variation in pressure placed on the pencil? When (and why) does the speed with which you write vary?
- What writing do you enjoy reading? Why? What would you rather not read? Why? When is your writing strongest? weakest? Why?
- Write a brief portrait of the journal writer. What does this person value in teaching? Include examples from the journal, perhaps illustrating main themes, or joys and frustrations or concerns.

As you peruse your journal or sections of it, look for insights and changes. Read a few excerpts from early writing and then read some more recent entries. If you have written for longer than a month or two, try analyzing the journal in three segments: beginning, middle, and end. Look at the content of your writing. Has this changed? One first-year teacher, for example, found that she focused on herself ("How can I get through this evaluation? How can I control David?") in early writing and on the children ("David seems better able to concentrate early in the morning. Julia's motor control is noticeably different than the other children's") in later writing. As a side note, this same teacher remarked that seminar discussions with other beginning teachers followed this same pattern: focus on me (teaching and survival) and then focus on the children (learning and development). Also, in both the journal and discussion there were changes in the types of concerns raised under each category. The teachers became more critical observers once "survival" was less of a concern. Figure 12–1 is an excerpt from a beginning teacher's journal reflections.

Just as venturing into broader contexts within which we teach can promote more comprehensive understandings of teaching, projecting backward and forward in time can facilitate planning and teaching. This is one of the reasons why the first year of teaching is so difficult, for the novice teacher has little understanding of the totality of teaching and how the year unfolds until he or she actually experiences it. Journal writing is especially important during this time because it makes reflection a conscious process. Writing slows down the rush of activity (keeping up) so that deliberate action can shape practice—thus helping the new teacher avoid merely responding to events as they happen.

To assist new teachers in learning from the first year of teaching and writing, I designed a final journal reflection paper (Appendix B). As the teachers thought about the year and reread their journals, I asked them to identify their major concerns and write about significant influences on them and their teaching (personal, family, school, community, society). They were also given a "Time-Events" line to reflect on the year. Figure 12–2 shows how two teachers used the sheet to describe the year.

FIGURE 12–1

**Excerpt from a
Beginning Teacher's Journal Reflections**

I found many differences in my writing throughout the year. Not so much in my handwriting but my attitude. I find that immediately following a weekend (time for "catch up" and organization) I am very optimistic. However throughout the week I become a little more pessimistic with each day. I also found that I continually speak of time management and organization. I am going to work this summer to develop a good system that works for me, along with a schedule to attempt to complete assignments before Saturday. My writings seem very defensive at the beginning of the year compared to now. I guess a little experience can really change your views. I also noticed that in the first few months my writings were very stressful and now I'm more at ease. When I was reading these I almost seemed like another person, and the things that seemed so important then aren't so important now. I'll bet if I kept track of everyday personal life I would see the same pattern.

FIGURE 12–2
Two Teachers' Time-Events Lines

JOURNAL ENTRY

Time-Events Line

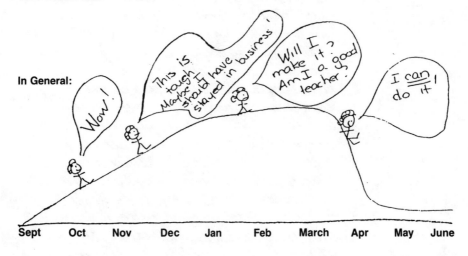

In General:

| Sept | Oct | Nov | Dec | Jan | Feb | March | Apr | May | June |

Me:

FIGURE 12–2

(continued)

JOURNAL ENTRY

Time-Events Line

In General:

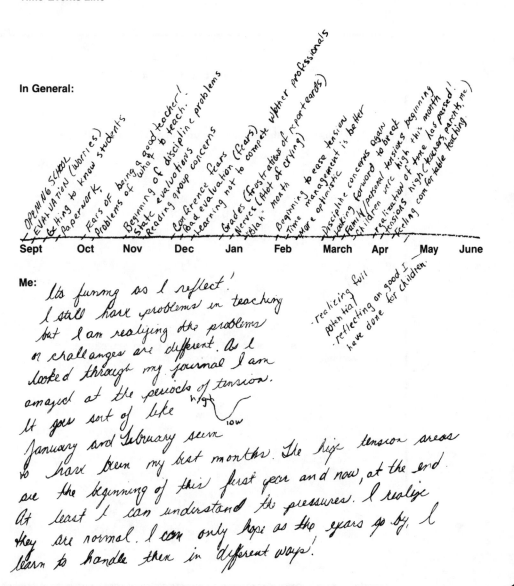

| Sept | Oct | Nov | Dec | Jan | Feb | March | Apr | May | June |

Me: Its funny as I reflect! I still have problems in teaching but I am realizing the problems or challenges are different. As I looked through my journal I am amazed at the periods of tension. It goes sort of like January and February seem to have been my best months. The high tension areas are the beginning of this first year and now, at the end. At least I can understand the pressures. I realize they are normal. I can only hope as the years go by, I learn to handle them in different ways.

Figure 12–3 is another journal entry sheet designed for reflecting on the year. It could also be used for describing the day or week or month. Another way to construct a portrait is to take excerpts from the journal and weave them into a portrait. Select one, two, or three unique or exemplary vignettes and weave them together by writing transitions where they are needed.

FIGURE 12–3

Images of the Year

JOURNAL ENTRY

As I think about the year these words and images come to me:

I made it –

As I look to future I see

New Ideas

More Ideas

Things for next year

If my year were a work of art (book, film, poem, sculpture, architecture, song, …), it would be:

(explain)

a 5 course gourmet dinner

because it contained a little of everything – parts that I liked (things I'll do again) and parts I didn't like (ideas I thought would be great, but weren't!)

like beets ... they're pretty but boy do they taste bad !

Several beginning teachers kept pictures and artifacts of their first year of teaching. Inserting these into the journal at appropriate places enabled the teachers to reconstruct the year with details that enabled them to recall specific and general experiences. These were invaluable in helping the teachers analyze the year and learn from their experiences. The pictures illustrated significant development in the children and in the teachers.

As Kate, an experienced teacher, read her journal and reflected on the school year, she began to think about how her teaching had changed over the years. Figure 12–4 is an excerpt from her journal reflections.

Russell Baker had a column in the *New York Times* Sunday Magazine entitled the "Sunday Observer." It was a one-page essay, usually humorous, on something that struck his fancy. One week he wrote about the agony of quitting smoking, the next about the proliferation of foreign-made products in the United States. This brings to mind another useful tool for learning from experience. Craig set aside each Sunday late afternoon for writing about a special topic. It was a time, as Russell Baker's column suggests, for musing on a topic of interest. Craig's journal was comprised of weekly writing punctuated by his Sunday essays on education. One way to analyze the journal is to look back at these essays to identify the topics over time. Did one have any relationship to another? What were the topics, purposes, and concerns embedded in the writing?

Like the Week-in-Review log sheet presented in chapter 8, weekly summaries can provide a rich source for reflection and analysis over the year or month or term. Many journal writers are surprised to find that some concerns remain constant over time. They find that patterns and themes emerge, and cycles recur. "Are Friday afternoons always wilder than Monday afternoons?" "I wrote about this same problem in different ways throughout the year!"

CONCLUDING COMMENTS

New questions and challenges keep popping up. Some of them are old and disguised so that they only appear to be new; others are genuinely new. Inquiry into one child's world opens opportunities for understanding other children; delving into issues in the profession can lead to personal insights and collaborative action. Probing life history and the challenges of practice, whether through biographical or autobiographical writing, case studies and action research, or simply curiosity, can lead to greater awareness, insight, and understanding of the social and historical circumstances that have influenced us and shaped today's schools and classrooms. In the process of naming ourselves and teaching, by telling our

FIGURE 12–4

**Excerpts from an
Experienced Teacher's Journal Reflections**

84

Apr. 28

How My Teaching Has Changed

Now	Then
I have more continuity in everything I do particularly curriculum wise.	I had "neat" ideas and fit them in where ever I could.
I'm more sure of my teaching philosophy.	I was the new young thing; "bright, but naive"
I don't feel nearly the need to prove my authority with children, parents or others at school	I needed that symbolic victory
I'm more involved with kids as I plan.	I planned with materials.
I rely more on myself.	I relied also on my aide.
I know each child better.	Earlier, though I had more children with the help of an aide, I still couldn't come up with an instant profile on a child as I can now.
I see patterns, trends, personality types, pick up on lots of subtle non-verbal clues.	

FIGURE 12–4
(continued)

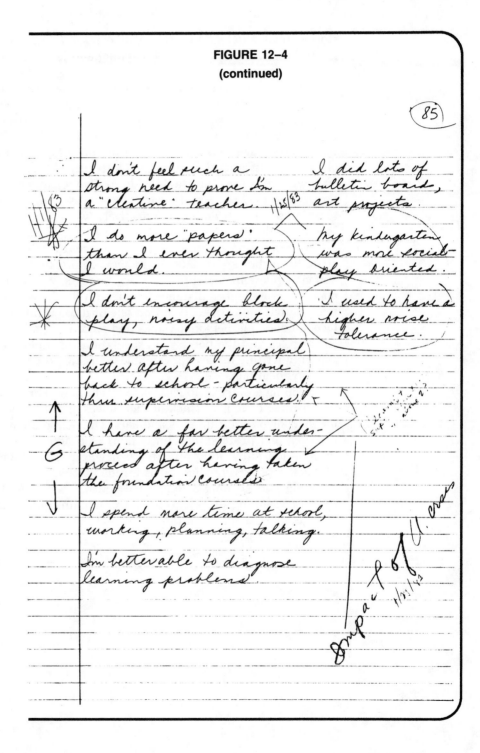

85

I don't feel such a strong need to prove I'm a "creative" teacher.

I did lots of bulletin board, art projects.

I do more "papers" than I ever thought I would.

My kindergarten was more social-play oriented.

I don't encourage block play, noisy activities.

I used to have a higher noise tolerance.

I understand my principal better after having gone back to school – particularly thru supervision courses.

I have a far better understanding of the learning process after having taken the foundation courses.

I spend more time at school, working, planning, talking.

I'm better able to diagnose learning problems.

stories in vignettes and portraits, we can see them more clearly and begin to describe our theories of teaching and learning: to theorize about practice.

"How do I know what I think until I see what I say?" It's in the actions and silences of saying something on paper, observing, reflecting, and discussing our thoughts, feelings, and ideas with others, that we learn. Holding a few of our daily experiences still long enough to acknowledge them takes acts of will, both the will to inhibit less important matters that clamor for our attention and the will to keep the selected topic in focus even when it is uncomfortable to do so. By focusing attention in writing, the author need not simply react to everyday happenings, but can learn to observe critically and more selectively "wheel in" the most appropriate "small minds" for making sense of experience (Ornstein 1988).

By unraveling and listening to the voices and themes of practice, we come to further appreciate the images, colors, and textures of teaching and view phenomena within broader contexts. We can learn how to gain enough psychological distance to detach from the action and emotion of many of our concerns. Given that one of the central difficulties teachers face is balancing personal values and feelings of adequacy with professional roles and the perceived expectations of others (Gates 1987), this aspect of writing makes it a valuable heuristic process for growth as well as a practical one.

Keeping a diary or journal is far from new. Throughout written history, people have kept track of themselves and told their stories, if only for their own inquiring eyes and ears. The deliberate attempt to explore personal and professional dimensions of practice in an organized way through journal writing probably is new, but it is a logical development in teacher professionalism. It is an integration and extension of lesson planning and keeping a diary. The journal becomes the author's own Book of Teaching—a celebration of mountains and tides that can cause even its most skeptical author to marvel.

Project Abstract:
Teacher Reflections on Classroom Life— An Empirical Base for Professional Development

The current study is designed to add to the knowledge bases of teaching and professional development. It is a phenomenological study of the classroom teacher and a group of seven teachers who are reflecting upon, writing about, and discussing their lives in classrooms over a one-year period. Teachers keep written diaries that contain their thoughts on daily events and serve as topics for discussion at weekly seminar sessions on teaching and professional development. Biweekly observations in each classroom are made by the researcher. Teachers were selected from seven school districts within a thirty-mile radius of Kent State University and include classroom levels from kindergarten through grade three in urban, rural, and suburban settings.

The research is built upon a conceptual framework that was generated in a previous study of teacher perceptions of professional growth and a perceptual approach to development (Holly 1977).

Major questions that are addressed include the following:

1. What do teachers think about on a daily and weekly basis? What are their problems and joys?
2. What are the events, interactions, and characteristics of the setting that have a significant impact upon their teaching and learning?
3. To what extent do activities and courses that are planned to assist them in their teaching actually help them?
4. What happens when teachers reflect consciously upon their teaching?
5. How do teachers help other teachers?
6. What do responses to these questions suggest for the improvement of support systems for professional development?

Data sources include diaries, transcriptions of seminar sessions, slides of each classroom and school, observations of participants' teaching and field notes, and informal interviews in each school (principals, children, parents, and staff members).

The phenomenological approach taken is one designed to enable the researcher to look at the classroom life of teachers from their perspectives and to describe the everyday and cumulative experiences that affect their and their students' lives in classrooms.

Research for this study was supported by the National Institute of Education, Knowledge Use and School Improvement, Research and Practice Unit, Washington, DC.

Reflections on Teaching: August 1986–June 1987

1. Take yourself back to the beginning of the school year. Use your memory, journal, lesson plan book, and any other artifacts you might have. Reread your journal. You might want to note reactions on a separate sheet of paper or with another color of ink right in the journal, as you go. Then, respond to the following questions:
   - What are your reactions to reading your journal?
   - What differences, if any, do you find in the writing? (Does the content change? the characteristics of writing? the quality or quantity? Do you focus on different aspects of practice? At the start of the year, were you focusing on different things: "How do I get a smoother transition from recess to reading?" In other words, do your questions and concerns change, and can you see this in your writing?)
   - Cite a few examples of critical incidents from this year. Why were they important?
   - What were some of the most important challenges and problems you faced? the biggest sources of frustration?
   - What were the most frequently written about topics in your journal?
   - What was important to your teaching but not written about?
   - What were some of the greatest sources of satisfaction or joy this year?
2. Write a brief portrait of yourself as a teacher. Include whatever you wish. You might want to include why you went into education, some philosophical statements of aims, examples or highlights of the first year, or hopes for next year. It is meant to be a short capsule of what you find interesting about yourself as a teacher this year. You might even write briefly about thoughts you had beginning (or before you began) teaching and how you think about it now. Your portrait might even be a group of excerpts from your journal woven together—amended or extended. Or take an excerpt and work this into a story about your teaching; use your writing as illustrations of your work.
3. Reflecting on the year, I learned about:
   - Teaching.
   - Myself as a teacher.
   - Children.
   - Administrators and administration.

- Curriculum planning and evaluation.
- Classroom management.
- Colleagues and resources.
- Professional and staff development.
- School systems.

4. What were some of the major influences on your teaching this year, both related to you and to the contexts within which you teach? (If you want to, use the log sheet from May 6, 1987.)

5. Advice to myself for next year:
   - Philosophy.
   - Aims.
   - Understanding and facilitating child development.
   - Planning: teaching and curriculum development.
   - Resources: people and materials.
   - Working with colleagues and parents.
   - Reflection and evaluation.
   - Personal, professional development.

References

Abbs, P. 1974. *Autobiography in Education*. London: Heinemann.

Ashton-Warner, S. 1966. *Teacher*. New York: Bantam Books.

——. 1967. *Myself*. New York: Simon & Schuster.

Asimov, I. 1986. In *Writers on Writing* by J. Winokur, 55. Philadelphia: Running Press.

Augustine, St. 1949. *The Confessions of Saint Augustine*. Trans. E. B. Pusey. New York: Modern Library.

Baker, R. 1982. *Growing Up*. New York: New American Library.

Baldwin, C. 1977. *One to One: Self-Understanding Through Journal Writing*. New York: M. Evans.

Ball, S. J., and I. F. Goodson, eds. 1985. *Teachers' Lives and Careers*. London: Falmer Press.

Benjamin, H. 1939. *The Sabre-Toothed Curriculum*. New York: McGraw-Hill.

Boswell, J. 1959. *Boswell's London Journal*. Ed. F. A. Pottle. London: Heinemann.

Burgess, R. G., ed. 1982. *Field Research: A Sourcebook and Field Manual*. London: George Allen & Unwin.

——, ed. 1985. *Issues in Educational Research: Qualitative Methods*. London: Falmer Press.

——. 1986. "Education as a Key Variable." In *Key Variables in Social Investigation*, ed. R. G. Burgess. London: Routledge and Kegan Paul.

Calkins, L. M. 1986. *The Art of Teaching Writing*. Portsmouth, NH: Heinemann.

Camus, A. 1979. *Albert Camus: The Essential Writings*. Ed. Robert E. Meagher. New York: Harper & Row.

Carroll, L. 1866. *Alice's Adventures in Wonderland*. London: Macmillan.

Cogan, M. 1973. *Clinical Supervision*. Boston: Houghton Mifflin.

Coles, R. 1967. *Children of Crisis: A Study of Courage and Fear*. Boston: Little, Brown.

——. 1970. *Erik Erikson: The Growth of His Work*. Boston: Little, Brown.

——. 1971a. *Children of Crisis: Migrants, Sharecroppers, Mountaineers*. Boston: Little, Brown.

——. 1971b. *Children of Crisis: The South Goes North*. Boston: Little, Brown.

——. 1977a. *Children of Crisis: Eskimos, Chicanos, Indians*. Boston: Little, Brown.

——. 1977b. *Children of Crisis: Privileged Ones: The Well Off and the Rich in America*. Boston: Little, Brown.

Coles, R., and J. H. Coles. 1980. *Women of Crisis II: Lives of Work and Dreams*. New York: Delacorte Press/Seymour Lawrence.

Combs, A. 1965. *The Professional Education of Teachers*. Boston: Allyn & Bacon.

Connelly, F., and D. J. Clandinin. 1983. "Studies in Personal Practical Knowledge: Image and Its Expression in Practice." Paper presented to the International Study Association on Teacher Thinking, Tilburg, Holland.

Conrad, J. 1953. *The Secret Agent: A Simple Tale.* Garden City, NY: Doubleday.

Cummings, E. E. 1962. *A Selection of Poems 1923–1954.* New York: Harcourt, Brace & World.

Darwin, C. 1877. "A Biographical Sketch of an Infant." *Mind* 2: 296–94.

Dewey, J. 1929. *My Pedagogical Creed.* Washington: Progressive Education Association.

Dickens, C. 1917. *David Copperfield.* New York: P. F. Collier & Son.

Dillard, A. 1987. *An American Childhood.* New York: Harper & Row.

Doctorow, E. L. 1984. *Lives of the Poets.* New York: Random House.

Dollard, J. 1935. *Criteria for the Life History.* New Haven: Yale University Press.

Easton, G. 1983. *Learning from Case Studies.* Englewood Cliffs, NJ: Prentice Hall.

Ebbutt, D. 1985. "Educational Action Research: Some General Concerns and Specific Quibbles." In *Issues in Educational Research: Qualitative Methods*, ed. R. G. Burgess. London: Falmer Press.

Eiseley, L. 1978. *The Star Thrower.* New York: Harcourt Brace Jovanovich.

Eisner, E. W. 1985. *The Educational Imagination: On the Design and Evaluation of School Programs.* 2d ed. New York: Macmillan.

Elbow, P. 1973. *Writing Without Teachers.* New York: Oxford University Press.

Elkind, D. 1983. *All Grown Up and No Place to Go: Teenagers in Crisis.* Reading, MA: Addison-Wesley.

Elliott, J. 1976. "Developing Hypotheses from Teachers' Practical Constructs." Mimeo. University of North Dakota.

———. 1981. "Action Research: A Framework for Self-Evaluation in Schools." TIQL working paper no. 1 (mimeo). Cambridge Institute of Education.

Elliott, J., and C. Adelman. 1973. "Reflecting Where the Action Is: The Design of the Ford Teaching Project." *Education for Teaching* 92: 8–20.

Erikson, E. 1950. *Childhood and Society.* New York: Norton.

———. 1958. *Young Man Luther: A Study in Psychoanalysis and History.* Austin Riggs Center, Monograph No. 4. New York: Norton.

———. 1969. *Gandhi's Truth: On the Origins of Militant Nonviolence.* New York: Norton.

———. 1975. *Life History and the Historical Moment.* New York: Norton.

Evans-Pritchard, E. E. 1973. "Some Reminiscences and Reflections on Fieldwork." *Journal of the Anthropological Society of Oxford* 4(1): 1–12.

Ferrucci, P. 1982. *What We May Be.* New York: St. Martin's Press.

Forster, E. M. 1985. *Commonplace Book.* Ed. Philip Gardner. Stanford, CA: Stanford University Press.

Fothergill, R. 1974. *Private Chronicles: A Study of English Diaries.* London: Oxford University Press.

Frame, J. 1982. *To the Is-Land: An Autobiography.* London: Women's Press.

France, A. 1922. *La Vie Litteraire.* 2d ed. Trans. A. W. Evans. New York: John Lane.

Frank, A. 1952. *Anne Frank: The Diary of a Young Girl.* New York: Doubleday.

Franklin, M. 1901. *My Brilliant Career.* Melbourne: Georgian House.

———. 1946. *My Career Goes Bung.* Melbourne: Georgian House.

———. 1963. *Childhood at Brindebella.* Melbourne: Angus & Robertson.

Freire, P. 1971. *Pedagogy of the Oppressed.* Trans. M. B. Ramos. New York: Herder and Herder.

Freud, S. 1961. *The Standard Edition of the Complete Psychological Works of Sigmund Freud.* Ed. J. Strachey. London: Hogarth Press.

Fuller, F. 1969. "Concerns of Teachers: A Developmental Characterization." *American Educational Research Journal* 6 (2): 207–26.

Gardner, J. 1963. *Self-Renewal: The Individual and the Innovative Society.* New York: Harper & Row.

Gates, J. 1987. *A Theatre of Contradictions: Dilemmas in the Role of an LEA Advisor.* Unpublished M. Ed. thesis, Durham University.

Goldhammer, R. 1969. *Clinical Supervision: Special Methods for Supervision of Teachers.* New York: Holt, Rhinehart & Winston.

Goodlad, J. 1984. *A Place Called School: Prospects for the Future.* New York: McGraw-Hill.

Goodson, I. F., and S. J. Ball. 1984. *Defining the Curriculum: Histories and Ethnographies.* London: Falmer Press.

Graves, D. 1983. *Writing: Teachers & Children at Work.* Portsmouth, NH: Heinemann.

Greene, M. 1973. *Teacher as Stranger.* Belmont, CA: Wadsworth.

———. 1978. *Landscapes of Learning.* New York: Teachers' College Press, Columbia University.

———. 1982. "A General Education Curriculum: Retrospect and Prospect—a Viewing." Paper presented at the American Educational Research Association Annual Conference, New York.

Grumet, M. 1979. "A Methodology of Self-Report for Teacher Education." *Journal of Curriculum Theorizing* 1(1):191–257.

———. 1980. "Autobiography and Reconceptualization." *Journal of Curriculum Theorizing* 2(2):155–58.

Gulick, J. 1977. "Village and City Fieldwork in Lebanon." In *Marginal Natives at Work: Anthropologists in the Field*, ed. M. Freilich, 89–118. New York: Wiley.

Hammarskjold, D. 1983. *Markings.* New York: Ballantine Books.

Heath, D. 1980. "Toward Teaching as a Self-Renewing Calling." In *Exploring Issues in Teacher Education: Questions for Future Research*, ed. G. Hall, S. Hord, and G. Brown. Austin: Research and Development Center for Teacher Education.

Holly, M. L. 1977. "A Conceptual Framework for Personal-Professional Growth: Implications for Inservice Education." Unpublished doctoral dissertation, Michigan State University.

———. 1983a. "Teacher Reflections on Classroom Life: Collaboration and Professional Development." *Australian Administrator* 4(4):1–4.

———. 1983b. *Keeping a Personal-Professional Journal.* Victoria: Deakin University Press. (2d ed. 1987.)

Holly, P., and D. Whitehead. 1984. *Action Research in Schools: Getting It into Perspective.* Classroom Action Research Network, Bulletin No. 6, Cambridge, England: Cambridge Institute of Education.

———. 1986. *Collaborative Action Research.* Classroom Action Research Network, Bulletin No. 7, Cambridge.

Horner, M. 1980. Foreword. In *Women of Crisis II: Lives of Work and Dreams* by R. Coles and J. H. Coles. New York: Delacorte Press/Seymour Lawrence.

Huebner, D. 1975. "Curriculum Language and Classroom Meanings." In *Curric-

ulum Theorizing: The Reconceptualists, ed. W. Pinar, 217–36. Berkeley: McCutchan.

Hulbert, M. K. 1983. "The Legend of Brady's Landing: Collection of Related Short Stories." Master's thesis. University of the State of California at Chico.

Jersild, A. 1955. *When Teachers Face Themselves*. New York: Bureau of Publications, Teachers College, Columbia University.

Kanin, R. 1981. *Write the Story of Your Life*. New York: Hawthorn/Dutton.

Kelley, E. C. 1947. *Education for What Is Real*. New York: Harper.

Kelly, A. 1985. "Action Research: What Is It and What Can It Do?" In *Issues in Educational Research: Qualitative Methods*, ed. R. Burgess. London: Falmer Press.

Kelly, G. 1955. *The Psychology of Personal Constructs*. New York: Norton.

Kemmis, S. 1985. "Action Research." In *The International Encyclopedia of Education: Research and Studies*, Vol. 1, 22–25. New York: Pergamon Press.

Kemmis, S., and R. McTaggart. 1981. *The Action Research Planner*. Victoria: Deakin University Press.

Kipling, R. 1930. "Baa Baa Black Sheep." In *The Best Short Stories of Kipling*, ed. R. Jarrell. Garden City, NY: Hanover House.

Knoblock, P., and A. Goldstein. 1971. *The Lonely Teacher*. Boston: Allyn & Bacon.

Kuhn, T. 1962. *The Structure of Scientific Revolutions*. Chicago: University of Chicago Press.

Laing, R. D. 1982. *The Voice of Experience*. London: Allen Lane/Penguin.

Lewin, K. 1948. *Resolving Social Conflicts*. New York: Harper.

Lewis, O. 1966. *The Children of Sanchez: Autobiography of a Mexican Family*. Harmondsworth: Penguin.

Lightfoot, S. L. 1983. *The Good High School: Portraits of Character and Culture*. New York: Basic Books.

Lippit, R. 1949. *Training in Social Conflicts*. New York: Harper.

Little, J. 1982. "Norms of Collegiality and Experimentation: Workplace Conditions of School Success." *American Educational Research Journal* 19(3): 325–40.

Loevinger, J. 1976. *Ego Development: Conceptions and Theories*. San Francisco: Jossey-Bass.

Lortie, D. C. 1975. *Schoolteacher: A Sociological Study*. Chicago: University of Chicago Press.

MacDonald, J., and R. Leeper, eds. 1966. *Language and Meaning*. Washington, DC: Association of Supervision and Curriculum Development.

McLoughlin, P. 1985. personal communication.

Macrorie, K. 1984. *Searching Writing: A Context Book*. Portsmouth, NH: Boynton/Cook.

Mallon, T. 1984. *A Book of One's Own: People and Their Diaries*. New York: Ticknor & Fields.

Marks, J., E. Stoops, and J. King-Stoops. 1978. *Handbook of Educational Supervision: A Guide for the Practitioner*. Boston: Allyn & Bacon.

Maslow, A. 1979. *The Journals of A. H. Maslow*. Monterey, CA: Brooks/Cole.

Merleau-Ponty, M. 1965. "Man and Adversity." In *Signs*, trans. R. C. McCleary, 242. Evanston: Northwestern University Press.

Merriam-Webster Dictionary. 1974. New York: Pocket Books.

Mezirow, J. 1981. "A Critical Theory of Adult Learning." *Studies in Adult Education* 32 (1):3–24.

Miller, H. 1964. *Henry Miller on Writing.* Selected by Thomas A. Moore. New York: New Directions.

Newman, K., P. Burden, and J. Applegate. 1980. "Helping Teachers Examine Their Long-Range Development." *The Teacher Educator* 15(4) (Spring):7–14.

Nias, J. 1983. "Learning and Acting the Role: In-School Support for Primary Teachers." Paper presented at the American Educational Research Association Meeting, Montreal.

———. 1984. "A More Distant Drummer: Teacher Development as the Development of Self." Mimeo. Cambridge Institute of Education, Cambridge.

O'Brien, K. 1943. *English Diaries and Journals.* London: William Collins.

Oja, S., and G. Pine. 1983. *A Two-Year Study of Teachers' Stages of Development in Relation to Collaborative Action Research in Schools.* Final report to the National Institute of Education, Durham, NH. September.

Ornstein, R. 1988. *Multimind: A New Way of Looking at Human Behavior.* London: Macmillan.

Osherson, S. 1980. *Holding on or Letting Go: Men and Career Change at Midlife.* New York: The Free Press.

Papalia, D., and S. W. Olds. 1975. *A Child's World: Infancy Through Adolescence.* New York: McGraw-Hill.

Pepys, S. 1893. *The Diary of Samuel Pepys.* Vols. I and II. Ed. H. B. Wheatley. New York: Random House.

Percy, W. 1954. *The Message in the Bottle: How Queer Man Is, How Queer Language Is, and What One Has to Do with the Other.* New York: Farrar, Straus and Giroux.

Peshkin, A. 1983. "The Odd Man Out: Observer in an Absolutist Setting." Mimeo.

Piaget, J. 1952. *The Origin of Intelligence in Children.* New York: International Universities Press.

Pinar, W., ed. 1975. *Curriculum Theorizing: The Reconceptualists.* Berkeley: McCutchan.

———. 1980. "Life History and Educational Experience." *Journal of Curriculum Theorizing* 2(2):59–212.

———. 1981. "Life History and Educational Experience." *Journal of Curriculum Theorizing* 3(1):259–86.

Plummer, K. 1983. *Documents of Life: An Introduction to the Problems and Literature of a Humanistic Method.* London: George Allen & Unwin.

Polanyi, M. 1967. *The Tacit Dimension.* Garden City, NY: Anchor Books.

Pollard, M. 1986. "Explorations in Search of Self: Journal Writing for Personal and Professional Development." Paper presented at the Eighth Conference on Curriculum Theory and Classroom Practice, Dayton. October.

Progoff, I. 1975. *At a Journal Workshop.* New York: Dialogue House.

The Random House Dictionary. 1967. Unabridged ed. New York: Random House.

Rappaport, R. N. 1970. "Three Dilemmas in Action Research." *Human Relations* 23:499–513.

Runyan, W. 1982. *Life Histories and Psychobiography: Explorations in Theory and Methods.* New York: Oxford University Press.

Sarton, M. 1973. *Journal of a Solitude.* New York: Norton.

Savary, L., et al. 1984. *Dreams and Spiritual Growth.* New York: Paulist Press.

Schatzman, L., and A. L. Strauss. 1973. *Field Research: Strategies for a Naturalistic Sociology.* Englewood Cliffs, NJ: Prentice-Hall.

Schön, D. 1983. *The Reflective Practitioner: How Professionals Think in Action.* New York: Basic Books.

Schubert, W. H. 1986. *Curriculum: Perspective, Paradigm, and Possibility.* New York: Macmillan.

Schwab, J. 1969. "The Practical: A Language for Curriculum." *School Review* 78: 1–23.

Scott-Maxwell, F. 1968. *The Measure of My Days.* New York: Alfred A. Knopf.

Sergiovanni, T. 1982. "Supervision and the Improvement of Instruction." In *Supervision of Teaching,* ed. T. Sergiovanni, vi–viii. Alexandria, VA: Association for Supervision and Curriculum Development.

Shaw, C. 1930. *The Jack Roller: A Delinquent Boy's Own Story.* Chicago: University of Chicago Press.

Shulman, L. 1987. "Knowledge and Teaching: Foundations of the New Reforms." *Harvard Educational Review* 57(1)(February): 1–22.

Simmons, L. 1942. *Sun Chief: The Autobiography of a Hopi Indian.* New Haven: Yale University Press.

Simons, G. F. 1978. *Keeping Your Personal Journal.* New York: Paulist Press.

Smith, L. M. 1984. "Ethnographic and Historical Method in the Study of Schooling." In *Defining the Curriculum: Histories and Ethnographies,* ed. I. Goodson and S. J. Ball. London: Falmer Press.

Smyth, W. J. 1983. "Teaching as Learning: The Approach of Clinical Supervision." Unpublished manuscript. Deakin University, Victoria.

———. 1984. *Clinical Supervision—Collective Learning About Teaching: A Handbook.* Victoria: Deakin University.

Spencer, D. 1985. *Contemporary Women Teachers: Balancing School and Home.* White Plains: Longman.

Sprinthall, N., and L. Sprinthall. 1980. "Adult Development and Leadership Training for Mainstream Education." In *Concepts to Guide the Education of Experienced Teachers,* ed. D. Corrigan and K. Howey. Reston, VA: Council for Exceptional Children.

Stenhouse, L. 1975. *An Introduction to Curriculum Research and Development.* London: Heinemann.

———. 1985. Cover page. In *Research as a Basis for Teaching: Readings from the Work of Lawrence Stenhouse,* ed. J. Rudduck and D. Hopkins. London: Heinemann.

Stillman, P. 1987. Personal communication.

Strong, G. T. 1952. *The Diary of George Templeton Strong.* 4 vols. New York: Macmillan.

Taylor, J. 1983. *Dreamwork.* New York: Paulist Press.

Thomas, L. 1975. *The Lives of a Cell: Notes of a Biology Watcher.* Toronto: Bantam Books.

Thomas, W. I., and F. Znaniecki. 1918–1920. *The Polish Peasant in Europe and America.* Chicago: University of Chicago Press.

Thoreau, H. D. 1961. *The Heart of Thoreau's Journals.* Ed. O. Shepard. New York: Dover.

Tripp, D. 1984. "From Autopilot to Critical Consciousness: Problematising Successful Teaching." Paper presented at the Sixth Conference on Curriculum Theory and Classroom Practice, Dayton. October.

Twain, M. 1961. *The Autobiography of Mark Twain.* New York: Washington Square Press.

Vaillant, G. 1977. *Adaptation to Life.* Boston: Little, Brown.

Vonnegut, K. 1981. *Palm Sunday.* New York: Dell.

Walker, A. 1982. *The Color Purple.* New York: Washington Square Press.

Walker, R. 1971. "The Social Setting of the Classroom: A Review of Observational Studies and Research." Unpublished M. Phil. thesis, Chelsea College of Science and Technology, University of London.

Waller, W. 1932. *The Sociology of Teaching.* New York: Russell & Russell.

Watts, A. W. 1951. *The Wisdom of Insecurity: A Message for an Age of Anxiety.* New York: Pantheon.

Waugh, E. 1976. *The Diaries of Evelyn Waugh.* Ed. M. Davie. Boston: Little, Brown.

Webb, S., and B. Webb. 1932. *Methods of Social Study.* London: Longmans Green.

Welty, E. 1983. *One Writer's Beginnings.* Cambridge, MA: Harvard University Press.

White, R. 1952. *Lives in Progress: A Study of the Nature of Growth of Personality.* New York: Dryden Press.

Wilhelms, F. 1973. Foreword. In *Clinical Supervision* by M. Cogan. Boston: Houghton Mifflin.

Williams, W. C. 1978. *I Wanted to Write a Poem.* New York: New Directions.

Woolf, V. 1978. *A Writer's Diary.* Bungay, Suffolk: Triad Granada.

Yin, R. K. 1984. *Case Study Research: Design and Methods.* Beverly Hills: Sage Publications.

Zinsser, W. 1983. *Writing with a Word Processor.* New York: Harper & Row.

———. 1985. *On Writing Well: An Informal Guide to Writing Nonfiction.* 3d ed., revised and enlarged. New York: Harper & Row.

Index